Strange But True

A collection of true stories from the files of FATE Magazine

One afternoon in November 1974 I was tending my grandchildren because my daughter Margaret Carter was ill with influenza. It was getting on toward two o'clock and time to pick up Daniel from Emerson School where he attended first grade.

I noticed young Jared playing with the slate and chalk I had bought that morning for his brother. I realize most toddlers will play with anything within reach but I wanted Daniel's gift to look like new when he got home from school. So I took the chalk away from Jared and planned to take the slate to the kitchen to wash off his scribbles.

But they were not scribbles. In chalk was a command: "Take me home, now." I grabbed the baby and hurried to Margaret's house two blocks away.

She didn't respond to my ringing the doorbell so I entered anyway. I smelled gas which was escaping from a faulty heater. I set Jared on the porch and dragged Margaret from the couch into the fresh air. She soon regained consciousness.

I thank God for Jared's automatic writing and for the urge to buy a slate and chalk that morning.

— *"Message in Chalk," page 90*

About the Editors

Corrine Kenner has worked as a writer, editor, and graphic designer since 1982. Her lifelong interest in the paranormal inspired her to earn a degree in philosophy from California State University, Long Beach. She lives in St. Paul, Minnesota, in a house frequently visited by spirits.

Craig Miller entered magazine publishing in 1986, and has written and edited magazines for industries including professional photography, veterinary medicine, marketing, and recreation. He also is a talented artist whose ink and watercolor illustrations have been published around the world.

How to Write to the Editors

If you wish to contact the editors or if you would like more information about this book, please write to them in care of FATE Magazine. Both the editors and the publisher, Llewellyn Worldwide, Ltd., appreciate hearing from you. Please write to:

FATE Magazine
c/o Llewellyn Worldwide, Dept. K 298-4
P.O. Box 64383
St. Paul, MN 55164-0383, U.S.A.

Please enclose a self-addressed, stamped envelope for reply. If you are outside the U.S.A., please enclose an international postal reply coupon.

Strange But True

*A collection of true stories
from the files of FATE Magazine*

**Edited by
Corrine Kenner and Craig Miller**

2003
Llewellyn Publications
St. Paul, Minnesota 55164-0383, U.S.A.

FIRST EDITION
Fourth printing, 2004

Cover design: Tom Grewe
Book design: Corrine Kenner
Editing: Corrine Kenner and Craig Miller

Cataloging-in-Publication Data:
    Strange But True: A collection of stories from the files of FATE
    Magazine / edited by Corrine Kenner and Craig Miller.

    p. cm.
    ISBN 1-56718-298-4 (trade paper)
    1. Parapsychology — Case studies. 2. Spiritualism — Case studies.

    I. Kenner, Corrine. 1964-   . II. Miller, Craig. 1961-   .
    III. Fate (Chicago, Ill.)
    BF1029.S77 1997
    133—dc21   97-29626
                                                                CIP

Llewellyn Publications
A Division of Llewellyn Worldwide, Ltd.
P.O. Box 64383, St. Paul, MN 55164-0383
http://www.llewellyn.com

Printed in the United States of America

CONTENTS

Voices of Warning 105

Visions of Death 117

Visits from the Dead 137

Ghost Stories   **223**

INTRODUCTION

I sat straight up in bed and yelled, 'The lights, the lights, do you see the lights?'" wrote Lise Milner of Los Angeles. After her strange sighting in the middle of the night, she related her experience in the January 1996 issue of FATE magazine. "My views certainly changed," she said. "More than ever, I believe that I was a witness to higher intelligence, and I can more realistically and sympathetically relate to the claims of others."

For almost 50 years, FATE has printed stories of paranormal encounters in "True Mystic Experiences" and "My Proof of Survival," two of FATE's most popular — and enduring — departments. The stories are amazing firsthand accounts, filled with all the details, emotions, and puzzling paranormal mysteries that only actual witnesses can provide. Though readers may find some of the stories in this book hard to believe, they are true. Each of the writers signed a notarized affidavit attesting that their stories happened exactly as they've described them.

When you read this book, you might even remember a time that you have experienced the paranormal yourself — whether it was déjà vu, synchronicity, or a premonition. It's a strange world we live in, and as Shakespeare wrote, "There are more things in Heaven and Earth, Horatio, than are dreamt of in your philosophy." These stories may confirm your philosophy — or give you a reason to reconsider it.

Strange But True poses many of the questions humanity has struggled with through the ages: What happens to us when we die? Can we communicate with the souls of loved ones who have passed on? Are there guardian angels? Can we travel through time?

But just as importantly, the book provides answers. It contains eyewitness, factual reports that can help us understand the true nature of paranormal subjects so often shrugged off by science. Written by ordinary people faced with extraordinary circumstances, the stories permit an up-close and personal examination of psychic warnings, miraculous healings, precognitive dreams, and the mysterious appearances of angels, aliens, and ghosts.

This book is not, however, a weighty tome intended to instruct the reader in the finer points of spirituality, philosophy, zoology, or astrology. The book is fun. We hope you enjoy reading it as much as we enjoyed editing it.

— *Corrine Kenner and Craig Miller*
St. Paul, Minnesota
June 1997

A BOOK OF MAGIC

*Shortly after FATE Magazine was founded in 1948, editor-in-chief
Charles Fuller issued a memo to his staff. His brief missive outlined his
vision for the magazine — a vision that has inspired FATE editors and
delighted FATE readers for 50 years. But more than that, it also
describes the nature of the accounts you'll find in this book. We hope
Strange But True conforms to Fuller's definition of "a book of magic."*

Here is the text of Fuller's memo, issued October 13, 1954:

P sychological and motivational studies applied to publications
have a lot of hokum about them, but I think you should both
ask yourselves: What is FATE all about?

I'm going to tell you what I think FATE is about.

I think FATE is a book of magic. When we were kids we
believed in fairies and brownies and ghosts and hobgoblins and miracles. I think FATE shows, or should show, that fairies and brownies and hobgoblins and miracles exist today.

When we write a story about the mind, all the direction of that
story and the efforts of that story should be in writing about the miracle of the mind — the magical accomplishments of that mind.

And that should be true of everything that appears in FATE.

In a world of materialism people have lost faith in magic. Yet
from that same materialistic world, some have re-created the basis
for a new belief in magic. The science that destroyed magic has
advanced to the point where belief in magic again becomes scientif-
ically possible.

It is FATE's job not only to point this out but to create an aura
of magical belief for its readers. I think we should reason this out
most carefully. We should weigh everything in the magazine from
this viewpoint.

An ancient civilization has magic because it shows what the mind
of man has accomplished. The mind, ESP, everything we run are subjects for FATE only if the editorial slant is toward that of magic.

Webster defines magic as "The art which claims or is believed to produce effects by the assistance of supernatural beings or by a mastery of secret forces in nature." I think our emphasis should be on the second part of this definition. We all believe that the magic we write about is produced by the secret forces in nature.

As far as we are concerned, we do not know what these forces are. But science seems to believe they exist (at least our science does) and I think that we all agree. Let's understand, then, that we are selling this kind of magic.

What is the importance of magic to FATE?

To the reader it re-creates the days of his childhood when he believed in magic. Usually the reader, at some time in his life, has doubted or has lost faith. FATE can restore that faith and belief in magic. We have done this with some readers and that is why they are so loyal. But we ought to be able to do it with more.

It is magical to believe in spirits, in survival, in the healing powers of the mind.

Survival and its belief are as much a part of magic as is religion. We do not emphasize religion very much; that is not our province. But from the purely scientific viewpoint, religion is magic.

The problem for us as editors, therefore, is to make FATE a magical book, convincing readers and potential readers of its faith, accuracy, and integrity in reporting on magical affairs.

Millions of people want to believe in magic. Somehow we've got to convince them FATE will help them toward that belief. And all of this points toward those most fundamental wishful thoughts that:

"My mind is all powerful; it can do anything."

"Man survives; I survive!"

"The mind heals; it accomplishes miracles."

"Many strange things are going on in the world which no one yet understands.'

"All these things enhance my faith, my powers, my chances of success and wealth and happiness."

— *Charles Fuller*

MIRACLES AND MYSTERIES

A translucent form came out of my body and slowly floated down to where Jim lay. When it got to him, it disappeared. At that moment, Jim raised his arms...
— *From Marie Scarborough's "Timber!," page 17*

S ome paranormal events are more difficult to categorize than others. A man drives his 18-wheeler down a highway that seems to compress time. A girl has a vision of her own funeral, and after her death, she is possessed by five spirits who attempt to revive her. A woman goes shopping and finds herself trapped on an elevator that takes her to another dimension. Paranormal phenomena don't come in neat bundles. Visions and visitations can overlap healings and hauntings, leaving the reader almost as awestruck as those who experienced the inexplicable events firsthand.

Timber!

In 1974, I had a cabin near Big Lake, Washington. Two of my trees were blocking my neighbor's view of the lake, so my friend Jim Kieffer offered to cut them down.

While my neighbor and I stood to one side and watched, Jim cranked up the chainsaw, notched one tree, and expertly felled it into the lake. Then he started to saw the second tree — without notching it first. We were horrified. We knew that his oversight could cost him his life.

We yelled out a warning, but he couldn't hear us over the noise of the chainsaw. "The tree will split!" we screamed.

I grabbed my neighbor's hand and pulled her out of harm's way. As we watched, the tree broke in two. Some of the tree landed in the lake but a large section still rose from the stump. Without thinking, Jim put his head under the split end, over the stump, and kept sawing. Within seconds, the tree fell straight down onto his head, apparently crushing it flat. His body didn't move and his arms hung lifelessly.

I couldn't move, either. I felt like I had turned to stone.

At that moment, a translucent form came out of my body and slowly floated down to where Jim lay. When it got to him, it disappeared. At that moment, Jim raised his arms, placed them on the trunk, and pulled his head out from between the stump and the tree. The tree itself never moved.

I rushed down to him. His face was ashen, but there was no blood or contusions. He refused to go to a hospital, so I drove him home and kept an eye on him all week.

The following Sunday, we went back up to my cabin, where a professional lumberjack was cutting the fallen tree into pieces. Jim's cap was still caught between the tree and the stump. I asked the lumberjack to retrieve it. To our amazement, the cap was full of blood and hair — even though there had been no sign of injury a week earlier.

I'm sure we witnessed a miracle.

— *Marie Scarborough, Ontario, California*
May 1997

I Was Lost in the Fourth Dimension

The recollection of an experience I had in the fall of 1934 still fills me with chills of apprehension. Mentally, I always refer to this event as The Depot, and I wonder what would have happened to me if, somehow, I had never come back.

I was a young girl. My husband was still my fiance and we lived in Chicago. We both were music students and had been to an afternoon concert. Finding we had ample time before keeping a dinner date with his family, we decided to browse around in a nearby music store. We took the elevator upwards and, once in the store, settled down to study the latest scores and literature. I was paging through a magazine when my fiance, Stan, nudged me, pointing to the clock; it was time to go.

As far as I can be sure, we both returned to the elevator, but in the crush on the way down we got separated in the crowd. On arriving at what I thought was the main floor, I tried to push my way out but was shoved back. The door closed again and we started down. I thought I could hear my fiance calling my name as the elevator descended below street level. Finally, I felt the familiar thud which marked the end of the line for old-fashioned elevators and the door opened once more. I was going to stay on and ride back up, but an unfriendly operator insisted "Everybody off!"

Leaving the car I was astonished to find myself in an immense place, a basement surely, but not of a downtown office building. There were boxes and crates stacked everywhere. Grainy, perspiring men pushed carts or rode little trucks loaded with trunks and baggage. My eyes searched the place and I discovered, in one corner, a large iron staircase, like a fire escape. Walking toward it, I thought I could see daylight above, so I hurried to climb upward.

When I reached the top, which was indeed above ground and in broad daylight, I was completely bewildered. There was no sign of the store I had left. Nothing else that should have been there was visible. There was nothing unusual in my surroundings, but the place was totally unknown to me. I was in a large railroad station!

Crowds of travelers hurried about. There were the usual signs,

"To Trains," "Waiting Room," "Lunch Counter," "Tickets." I was so engrossed with my surroundings that I almost knocked down one poor woman. I apologized, but she hadn't even noticed me. I could see no signs of trains arriving or departing and no timetables. I was curious (an understatement) to know where I was.

Just then, an announcer's voice rose above the din to read off a long string of destinations. I have seldom been able to understand railroad announcers, however, and of his message I caught not one word. Wandering around confusedly, I finally sighted the information booth. There was a long line and I joined it. I felt foolish about having to ask where I was, but when I reached the girl and asked my question, she seemed completely unaware of my existence. This was the last straw and I hurried away.

I followed the wall until I saw a "To Seventh Street" sign and went outside into the open air. I still had no idea where I was. It was a beautiful day, with a cloudless blue sky that would have seemed like mid-summer had not the leaves on the great trees along the avenue already turned gold, crimson, and orange. There was a new red brick building going up across from the station. It looked like it might be a church. There were many people out on the street, all looking healthy, pleasant, and contented. I smiled at some of the passersby but received only blank stares. I heard friendly voices but couldn't understand a word. The place seemed so normal that I scarcely was frightened. But who in such a situation could be anything but confused and perplexed?

Wandering aimlessly along the street, I noticed a blond boy ahead of me, probably in his teens, standing in the center of the sidewalk and staring in all directions. Nearing him, I stepped to one side to pass, but as I did so, he smiled eagerly, and reached out to touch my arm as if to see if I was real. I stopped and smiled back.

He said haltingly, "I guess they let you off at the wrong stop, too." I immediately understood. However fantastic, the same thing had happened to both of us. Our mutual plight created a bond. We continued together down the broad avenue.

"This is weird," he said. "I was playing tennis back home and went to the locker room to change my shoes. When I came out I was in that depot."

"Where is 'home?'" I asked.

"Why, Lincoln — Lincoln, Nebraska, of course." He sounded puzzled.

"But I started this trip in Chicago!" I told him.

We walked on, discussing everything we had ever heard or read of time travel, teleportation, and other space dimensions. But neither of us knew much of this sort of thing and we didn't get far.

After a while the street became less crowded. Ahead the road sloped downhill. Soon the town was behind us. We were in open country and we saw the deep blue water of a lake or ocean ahead. It was a welcome distraction. We raced down the hill and out onto the sandy beach where we flopped down on some large rocks to catch our breath. It was really lovely there, warm and fresh. The sun was dipping toward the water on the horizon now, so we assumed that west was that direction.

As we watched the sun drop we noticed a large sandbar not too far out. I thought I heard voices coming from there. Suddenly, I heard someone calling my name and, as I grew accustomed to looking into the bright sunlight, I saw with great surprise that one of the girls on the sandbar was my fiance's sister. There were others with her and they all waved and shouted again.

My newfound friend jumped up in excitement. "But this is wonderful!" he said. "Maybe they are some kind of connection or link." He searched for the right words and, as he talked, he scrambled out of all his clothes but his tennis shorts. "I'm going out there," he exclaimed. "They see us! They know you! It's not far, and I can make it in a few minutes."

He dove into the waves and swam off. With an inner excitement, I watched him go. He shouted back occasionally and swam on. The figures remained on the bar and their voices still reached me. But as he swam a queer thing happened. Try as he might, he could get no nearer to the sandbar. Then gradually the bar seemed to grow more distant. Finally he turned and swam back to shore where he dropped onto the sand in total discouragement. There seemed nothing to say; when we looked out again the bar had disappeared. There was no fog, no obscuring mist, and while the sun was quite low in the sky, it was still very light. The sandbar had merely vanished.

I can't imagine what we would have done next but suddenly I was enveloped in darkness. I felt as if I floated in space and then I was back on the stool in the music store! The magazine was still spread out before me. A clock was striking and the clerks were tidying up the counters, preparing to close. I looked around for my fiance, fully expecting to see him there, but he was not in sight. I decided the best thing to do was to go straight to his home. This time I walked down the stairs!

When I got to my destination, my fiance opened the door. He certainly looked relieved. He said he'd lost me on the elevator. After stepping out on the main floor he had been unable to locate me. Thinking I had gotten off on some other floor, he had waited a while and then finally decided to go home.

The rest of the family was already in the dining room and we followed them without further discussion. When I entered, I was more than a little surprised to see Stan's sister with the same friends I had seen on the sandbar.

She smiled as she said, "We saw you in town but you were so engrossed in each other you didn't even hear us!"

— *Miriam Golding, Chicago, Illinois*
September 1956

A Debt Paid

One day in 1952 a Navy flyer, William Riordan, was driving home from the Naval air base where he was stationed when he noticed that cars on the road ahead were slowing down. As he approached, he saw that they were avoiding something lying near the narrow pavement. When he came alongside he observed that it was a man prone on the ground.

While other drivers blasted their horns in objection to his slowing down traffic to help what they called "a sleeping drunk," he pulled his car off the road and stopped to investigate. He found that the man had a large scalp wound that couldn't be seen from the road. After giving the man first aid, the flyer sent for an ambulance. When it had taken the man away, he went on home and forgot the incident.

Several months later the pilot was flying over the same area in a blinding snowstorm. The air intakes on three of the plane's engines became clogged with snow, causing a power failure. The plane crashed in a woods near the air base.

When the Navy ambulance arrived at the scene, they found the pilot hanging by his legs from a jagged piece of steel. The sharp edges had cut through his legs to the bones, but a man was standing under the flyer, holding him up, so his legs would not be completely torn off by the weight of his body. The man said he had been supporting the pilot like that for about an hour.

After they cut the flyer away from the wreckage, he regained consciousness for a time and discovered that the man who had saved his legs was the one he had aided alongside the road.

— *Raymond C. Otto, Chicago, Illinois*
June 1959

The Language of the Heart

My grandparents lived in the northern part of Missouri during the late 1800s. At that time a steady flow of people was still migrating west by wagon train.

One day, a lone wagon came down the dirt road in front of my grandparents' farm. In the wagon were a man, a woman and two small children.

Pulling on the horses' reins, the man stopped his team and the dust settled down around them. Always thrilled to see company, Grandfather and Grandmother hurried to meet them.

"We're lost!" the man said to my grandfather. "We were with a wagon train but had to stop for a while because of the children. The other wagons kept on going, and somewhere along the way we must have taken a wrong turn — we haven't seen them at all today!"

Grandfather asked them to stay for a while, but the man said they were in a hurry to catch up with the others. So Grandfather gave them instructions on how to get back to the main road. With smiles and waves, the family in the wagon left.

"You weren't very talkative, for once," Grandfather said to his wife. Grandmother, who was never at a loss for words, had been strangely quiet. She frowned and said, "I didn't know you spoke German!"

"German? I don't speak any foreign languages," Grandfather said. "What are you talking about?"

"Well, I don't know for sure what language it was, but it sure sounded like German to me. That's why I wasn't saying anything. I couldn't understand what you and those people were talking about!"

My grandparents always told this story with awe. How did it happen? How had Grandfather been able to converse in a language that he didn't even know?

We never knew if the lost family caught up with the wagon train and safely made it to their destination, but my grandfather had done what he could by extending his help and friendship.

I think when you have love and compassion for others, anything can happen. Even the amazing ability to speak another language!

— *Cecilia Elkurd, Bentonville, Arkansas*
May 1997

The Phantom Train

The peace and quiet of the late winter night, a full moon riding high, belied the holocaust of World War I then at its height in Europe.

My mother-in-law Ruth Stevens and her younger son Charles were living with my husband Theodore and me in our home in Baudette, Minnesota, near the Canadian border. Ruth's older son Edward was in the British armed services but he had written that he was leaving Liverpool for the United States and we would hear from him when he arrived. He was due any day. Thus we were very concerned with the daily arrival of mail and the train from Winnipeg.

On this particular night, however, we had learned there was trouble on the railroad and there would be no train. About 10 o'clock that night, Ruth and I were looking through our wide north window and saw the headlights of the southbound passenger train glimmering in the distance. The tracks were less than a quarter-mile from the house and the trains always were clearly visible to us — but we were a little surprised to see this one. However, we concluded that the trouble on the railroad had been cleared up.

We watched the oncoming lights, dazzling bright against the whiteness of the hard-packed snow. Then a strange thing happened. The locomotive slowed and came to a full stop, headlights shining and all coaches lighted up. We both remarked that the shades on the coach windows were halfway down and in the brightness of the lights, the seats could be seen clearly. There wasn't a soul sitting in any of those seats! Not a passenger, not a conductor, not a trainman could be seen in the whole length of the train.

It was eerily quiet, as if the whole world suddenly had come to a standstill. As we watched, the headlights blinked several times as if conveying a message. We waited for the train to start but it remained stationary. For about 10 minutes we puzzled over the odd incident, wondering what had stalled the locomotive.

In the morning my brother-in-law Charles ran to the post office as soon as it opened … and came flying back to say the train never came in at all. He had learned it would be noon before the train came since it hadn't left Winnipeg until 10 o'clock the night before.

But we saw it! Ruth and I had seen the stalled train at 10 o'clock the night before. Then we remembered the half-drawn shades and the empty seats. What did it all mean?

Ruth waited in vain for another letter from her son Edward. We never saw or heard from him from that day to this.

Was there a connection between his disappearance and the phantom train?

— *Mabel Stevens, Fort Myers, Florida*
May 1968

Possessed in New England

I n the late 1800s, 17-year-old Susie Smith, daughter of Dr. Green-leaf Smith, was the organist at Webster Hall in Lawrence, Mass-achusetts. She was a popular girl with a large circle of friends. While visiting her sister who lived at the corner of Cedar and Franklin Streets in Denmark, Maine, the girl took sick. On a Wednesday she awakened from a deep sleep, and said, "Father, I've attended my own funeral!"

Susie described the funeral, told of singing, giving the names of the hymns she had heard. Her father, mother, brother and sister lis-tened to the grim recital. The sick girl was perfectly rational during the remainder of the day but about six o'clock in the evening she had violent spasms. A paleness spread over her face. She became speechless, her eyes closed, and she died. The grief-stricken family wept around the death bed.

Many minutes had elapsed when, suddenly, to the indescribable surprise of everyone in the room, a deep, gruff voice spoke from the parted and moving lips of the dead girl.

"Rub both of her arms as hard as you can," the strange voice commanded.

The startled relatives obeyed. They rubbed and massaged the limp arms until a different voice ordered, "Raise her up."

Dr. Smith tenderly raised the body of his daughter to a sitting position, supporting the pitiful form from behind. The girl began to breathe. Now a voice different from the preceding two spoke, "If I could move her legs around so that I could set her up on the foot-board, she'd be all right."

The doctor was attempting to carry out this odd suggestion when he and the body of the girl were lifted from their positions together and both placed upon the foot-board by some unseen power.

The young girl's body now was possessed by still another intel-ligence, one that was cheerful, lively and not too unlike its original occupant. The doctor was about to ask if the girl's body hadn't bet-ter be laid back when the unseen force again lifted them backward, he to his feet, she to her original position on the bed, apparently as dead as before.

Minutes elapsed and the bewildered family waited sadly, uncertainly. Finally a fifth, mild voice started a conversation that continued for three hours. The voice admitted that the body had been controlled by "spirits." After the three hours, the girl slipped into a trance-like sleep. The next morning the girl's eyes opened and a sixth, unfamiliar voice asked, "Who am I?" The distraught father answered, "You are Susie Smith."

"No I ain't!" objected the voice. "Susie Smith died last night." The controlling influence voiced this opinion off and on during the rest of the day. That night the girl again was placed in a trance. Friday morning, the body underwent several changes and severe fainting spells were noted by the weary family. By noon the body was again quite dead.

The next morning, convinced that his daughter was gone at last, Dr. Smith had the body prepared for burial and removed to a room on the lower floor of the house. The saddened family gathered to decide whether to carry the dead girl back home for interment in Lawrence, or to bury the remains in Maine where she had died.

They were discussing this problem in hushed tones when, they swore later, an apparition of Susie Smith walked with plainly heard footsteps into the dimly lighted room. She said to them, "Right on the School Hill. Right on the side of the road." Then the apparition dissolved.

The family respected the choice of the apparition of Susie and in Denmark, Maine, Susie Smith was buried on the schoolhouse hillside. Six different personalities had temporarily occupied the dead body of Susie Smith in the presence of her astounded and grieving family.

— *Roy M. Frisen*
November 1954

The Flaming Curse

At two years of age my niece Pammy was an unusual child in many ways. Her bright red curls matched her personality and she was so intelligent she seemed older than her years. And she was a happy child — until her parents moved to a new home.

Connie and Dan had been delighted to locate a huge old house in Terre Haute, Indiana, with spacious bedrooms to house their growing family. Pammy was the fifth child and another was expected soon.

On moving day Pam's parents were alarmed to find a smoldering teddy bear in the attic of their new home but in the confusion of getting settled it had been promptly forgotten. Later events, however, made it seem like a significant omen.

In this house Pammy began having severe nightmares and visions, which everyone put down to an overactive imagination. Often in the wee hours of the morning, clutching her beloved rag doll, Pammy would come whimpering to her mother's bed.

"Mommy, he's pushed me out of bed again. He won't let me sleep and he's trying to take my dolly!"

At other times in the middle of the day Pammy would rush into the kitchen exclaiming, "Mommy, he pulled my hair and pinched me!" She could not explain who "he" was but she sounded is if it always was the same person and never a female. Once she told us her pesky visitor was big and old like "Pappy" (her pet name for her great-grandfather) who was about 70 years old.

At times these experiences were so upsetting that Pammy would be near hysteria; perspiration would mingle with the tears streaming down her face. At other times she passed "his" visits off with a shrug of her shoulders and refused to discuss them.

Connie and Dan decided that Pam was overstimulated by television or perhaps playing alone too much. She needed more companionship to discourage such alarming flights of fancy. Their solicitude, however, did not keep Pammy from awakening terror-stricken in the night.

Then, one sunny afternoon in March 1961, the unseen

tormentor nearly killed Pammy. She was standing in the center of the dining room when suddenly her panicky screams filled the air. Connie ran to her — to find Pammy's entire tiny body on fire! The flames leaping from the hem of her skirt engulfed her completely.

She suffered horrible disfiguring burns over 75 percent of her body requiring months of hospitalization and many skin grafts. In her torment of pain and drug-induced nightmares Pammy never once cried — but often she repeated, "Please, Mommy, don't let him hurt me again."

Careful investigation of the room where Pammy stood revealed nothing to account for the blaze. But while Pammy hovered between life and death in Saint Anthony's Hospital I heard a strange story, one that I believe explains the tragic occurrence.

I was working as a nurse's aide in the hospital. In the small coffee shop there it was not unusual to share a table with a complete stranger. One day I was seated with an elderly nurse's aide I had not previously met and as usually happens among hospital staff we were discussing our patients and complaining about the particularly nasty ones. I'll never forget her words as she unwittingly disclosed the mystery surrounding my sister's home and Pammy's accident.

"Of all the nasty people in the world," she said, "I had a neighbor who had everyone beat — old Mr. Clayton. I'll never forget that old man. He hated everything, kids most of all. In fact, he swore that if any child ever moved into his house, the parents would be sorry. He was really wild. If anyone could come back and haunt a house, it would be him. He died last year, a horrible death, and I think he deserved it." She paused to sip her coffee, then continued, "He burned to death in his bed." I felt a sickening lurch in the pit of my stomach. I had to ask, "Where did Mr. Clayton live?"

Yes, George Clayton had lived in Connie's big old house! Further questions elicited the information that Mr. Clayton's deathbed had been in the room Connie and Dan used for a dining room, exactly where Pammy had been burned.

Could all this be sheer coincidence? Or did a bitter old man wreak vengeance from the grave?

— *Judith E. Dixon, Safety Harbor, Florida*
March 1972

The Ghost Highway

In 1994 I drove a truck for a Phoenix-based company. One night I was pulling a load of minivans from Louisiana to Phoenix in an 11-ton Chevy with a 48-foot trailer. The truck was really acting up. It just seemed to be fighting me and falling apart. I didn't think it would get to Phoenix. When I got to El Paso I stumbled into the Petrol Truck Stop. I was tired, my head hurt, and my bad arm was throbbing.

I drank some coffee and talked with some of the other truckers. I knew that I should rest, but I was too anxious about getting home. When I left the truck stop I checked my odometer, recorded the reading, and took off. I saw an "Exit Three" sign for Highway 13. Something told me to take it.

I couldn't believe my luck. There was no traffic at all. The road was like a clear white ribbon. The pavement was smooth and even my truck was running smoothly, almost like new. There was no scenery, no road markers. All I passed were three old Indian cemeteries. I figured that I had at least a seven-hour trip ahead of me, so I was glad that I had a good road and my rig was doing all right.

My head even felt better so it didn't bother me that there were no exits for truck stops or anything else. Even so, I couldn't help wondering about Highway 13. I had heard that if a trucker going from El Paso to Phoenix was really in trouble he would find himself on Highway 13 and be protected on his way home. I couldn't help but remember other truckers who said that they had traveled the "Ghost Highway." One had been violently ill as he came into El Paso, but he had been determined to get home to Phoenix. Once in Phoenix doctors discovered that he had suffered a heart attack but still safely drove the 412 miles before collapsing.

I looked out the window and there to the left, sitting quietly on top of a flat rock, was a huge, pure white wolf. It made no effort to move, but stared at me with piercing green eyes. I had barely passed the wolf when I came across my first road sign. I couldn't believe what it said: "Arizona state line, nine miles." I had been on the road for less than two hours.

Soon I came across the only exit I had seen off Highway 13. A sign read, "Phoenix, 18 miles." I pulled into my shop exactly two and a half hours after leaving El Paso. The trip usually takes seven hours. By the time I went up 35th Avenue in Phoenix, the truck was acting up again. My mechanic did not understand how I had driven it 412 miles, and neither did I, but I will always be grateful for Highway 13 — the Ghost Highway.

— *John Gerzabek, Phoenix, Arizona*
March 1997

The Talking Toys

In 1994, my son George, his wife Tina, and their four children lived with me while their home was under construction. Every night before bed, my son would make sure all the outside doors were locked and secure. One night, I heard the front door open and shut, as if someone had come into the house. I got up to investigate only to find the front door locked. I checked the bedrooms: Everybody was in bed asleep. I thought I was just hearing things, so I went back to bed and fell asleep.

At 3:00 A.M. I was awakened by strange noises coming from my grandson Sean's bedroom. When I opened his bedroom door, a rush of cold air brushed past me.

I couldn't believe what I saw next: All four of the nine-year-old's talking "Power Ranger" toys were turned on. I moved quickly to turn them off, much to his relief. "Grandma," he said, "they've been talking for so long." He said they had gone on by themselves hours before, but he was so frightened he couldn't get out of bed to alert anyone. The next morning, he was still so shaken that we threw the toys away.

Later, my son said he hadn't heard any noise the night before, but that on previous nights he had heard doors open and shut and closet doors sliding. He would investigate, only to find no one else awake in the house.

I consulted a psychic friend of mine. She gave me a formula to clear the house of spirits. It is quiet now, but my grandson will still not stay overnight with me.

— *Elizabeth Thomas, Mesa, Arizona*
March 1997

"Prove it to Me!"

Claude Brown was a 16-year-old stockboy who worked in a shoe store I co-managed in Chicago back in 1979. He was aware of my involvement and interest in parapsychology and meta-physics, but he preferred to call it witchcraft.

Part of his daily routine consisted of teasing me about my beliefs. Declaring he had no such superstitions about anything, he'd further taunt me by saying, "Come on — try to do something to me to prove it."

We'd banter on a daily basis but I'd refuse to take the bait. Trying to explain to him the difference between witchcraft and psi fell on deaf ears.

One day he leaned on my desk and with a mischievous grin on his face he insisted I do something to convince him of my witch's abilities.

We stared at each other for a few seconds and I nodded my head in agreement.

"Okay, Claude," I said as I reached for a pencil and paper. "I'm going to write something on this paper, seal it in an envelope and lock it in my desk drawer. Let's see if anything happens."

He walked away, chuckling at my naiveté. He thought he had surely put one over on Mrs. K.

Weeks passed. Claude became less and less abusive about the subject matter. I noticed that he would arrive at work at various times with either a bandage on his hands or bandages placed in different areas. He'd sometimes stare at me in a questioning manner but wouldn't say anything. It was a bitterly cold day as only

Chicago weather can get when Claude, working in the stock room, was stung on his hand by a bee.

He stormed into my office. "All right, Mrs. K. I don't know what you wrote down, but my hands have been hurting me ever since. Whatever it is, will you please stop it?"

I opened the desk drawer and handed him the sealed envelope. After he opened it he gave me an odd look and walked away.

The words on the paper stated, "Whenever you have an evil or wrong thought it will be reflected with an injury to your hands. You are in complete control over this situation."

I think we were both more than just surprised by the outcome.

— *Irene Krawitz, Glenview, Illinois*
April 1991

Satan in the Corner

I grew up in Puerto Rico, in a small farming community called Las Carolinas. Back in June 1991, a string of mysterious events originated in the corner of my bedroom.

At the time, I was 18 and I was a big fan of Satanic rock music. My walls were covered with Satanic posters. But even though I was a Satanic rock fan, I never missed a single night of praying to God and the Virgin Mary.

The last thing I saw before I fell asleep each night was the corner of my room. For at least two weeks, I dreamed of that corner, over and over. One day, a strange figure appeared in my dreams: a man, dressed all in black, with a black shroud obscuring his face. As the nights progressed, the dreams continued, and in each dream the man grew increasingly violent. He would come over to my bed, lift my legs, and slam them hard against the bed.

I believed it was only a dream. One night, however, I woke up after the dream. It was 4:00 A.M., so I decided to get up for the day. Suddenly the strange figure appeared again. He stopped next to my bed, looked at me, and slammed both my legs against the bed. I panicked. I knew I wasn't asleep. Just as in the dreams, the figure disappeared.

The next morning I told my father about the strange events. He gave me a small statue of the Virgin Mary, which I put on the window sill next to my bed.

That night I had the same dream, but on the following night the strange figure decided to put an end to his nightly visits. "He's going to take my soul," I thought.

I tried to open my eyes, but I felt two hands holding them closed. I knew it was the Virgin Mary, blocking my view of what was happening.

"It's a war for my soul," I thought. I heard metallic sounds above me, like swords clanging. The noise lasted for about a minute. Then my eyes were free of the strange hands that were forcing them shut. When I heard the sounds of bells ringing peacefully, I realized that the nightly visits had stopped for good.

I believe the strange figure was Satan, claiming me because I listened to Satanic music. I thank God and the Virgin Mary for saving me.
— *Alex Saldaña, Caguas, Puerto Rico*
January 1996

Wreath of Feathers

Many times during my boyhood I heard older people talk about wreaths of feathers being found in the pillows on which someone had died. They seemed to feel this indicated that person had gone to heaven. I wondered if it was true because it seemed they always had heard of someone else who had seen such a wreath and never had seen one themselves.

One day when my half-brother, Luther, and I were stripping tobacco, we suddenly heard my mother screaming at the top of her voice. We couldn't imagine what had happened. At first we thought the house was on fire. But at last we got her quieted down so she could tell us what it was all about.

Still crying, but not so hysterically, she told us she had found a wreath of feathers in the pillow on which my seven-year-old brother, Ernest, had died.

At long last I got to see one of those wreaths of feathers I had heard so much talk about. It was round, about three and one half inches across, and just about one inch thick. All the feathers circled around with the quills pointing in the same direction. I doubt if mortal hands could have made one as perfect as this feather wreath was.

We kept this wreath of feathers for 20 years or longer. The last time I saw it, it was still intact. Not a feather was out of place. So I learned such wreaths are more than hearsay, and I hope Ernest is in heaven.

— *Chester B. Gillespie, Corinth, Kentucky*
August 1964

Shadows on the Wall

When my sister noticed the shadow of a woman on the dining room wall last March, her son remarked that the shadow resembled her. That night she realized her son was right, and she dreamed that she was trapped inside the wall at the spot where the shadow was. It seemed that some powerful force was holding her there so she could not move.

The next morning she again examined the shadow on the wall. Then, on impulse, she decided to check the rest of the wall. She removed a mirror that hung to the left of the shadow. Clearly revealed behind the mirror was another shadow, many times larger than the first. It was the shadow of a devil. This devil had an animal's head that looks like a cross between a rabbit and a donkey. The shoulders and body extend to just below the chest, and resemble a giant man. There was one eye in the head of the devil, a very evil eye, and it seemed alive.

A week after this discovery, her 18-year-old son disclosed that 13 years before he had been molested by his stepfather.

On March 20, my sister called me over to see the shadows on the wall. At my suggestion she splashed holy water on the wall. Then she soaked some paper towels in the holy water and rubbed them back and forth over the shadows. We waited while the old, faded, tan-colored wallpaper dried. The shadows were still there, and the devil's eye glared even more defiantly.

The shadow forms are darker than the rest of the paper and have a pale yellow outline. Three times my sister has scrubbed the walls with soap and water, and each time the shadows have returned, a little faded but still visible. The evil eye of the devil, however, has faded.

After the last washing, though, the devil's head spouted two more sets of eyes, one pair resembling human eyes, the other more animal-like, closely set, sad and watchful and quite evil looking.

What is the significance of these shadows? A shadowed imprint of the stepfather in an obscene pose has appeared on his bedroom ceiling. We believe the shadows relate to what happened to the boy. My sister went to the police, but they claim the crime cannot be punished after so many years of silence. Because of illness she cannot move away. Vengeance and justice must be left to Almighty God.

— *N. M., Los Angeles, California*
March 1965

Back in Time?

In August 1964, my friend V. Stephens and I spent a holiday in Bruges, Belgium. One day we toured the town in a horse-drawn cab and stopped at several places of interest, among them the Old People's Almshouses.

We found ourselves in a square surrounded on three sides by cottages with a plot of untilled ground in the center. Elderly people were sitting about talking and making lace at little tables. One lady invited me into her cottage and offered me orange squash. My friend bought a lace-edged handkerchief. We visited the chapel which was on the left-hand side of the place, halfway down the block, and then we said farewell and left.

We vacationed in Bruges for a week and before we departed, we decided to have another horse-cab ride. We asked the driver to stop at the same Almshouse. He took us through the familiar gateway and we found ourselves once again in the square.

But the scene was different from the one we remembered. There were no people about. We saw no lacemakers, even though it was a warm day. The large untilled plot of ground now held a mass of fully grown flowers and vegetables. We went to look for the chapel but it was not there. Eventually we found it at the end of the block.

We met an attendant and told him that we thought the chapel had been on the left, in the center of the left-hand row of cottages. "Oh, yes, it used to be," he replied, "but it's been moved."

We left somewhat mystified. Where were the people and the lacemakers? Why was every door shut when previously each had stood hospitably open? How was it that the open field in the center had been cultivated when a week ago it had been bare? And how did the chapel get moved and rebuilt in the space of a few days? We thought at first that there must have been two old people's homes, the second different from the first. But it seemed unlikely that two almshouses along the same road would be built almost exactly alike, and we had asked the driver of the cab to take us to see the almshouse we had visited before.

The only other explanation, incredible as it may have been, was that somehow we had stepped back in time during the first visit and had seen the lacemakers who once had lived there. We had gone back to a period before the chapel had been moved and the plot of land tilled.

Skeptics might say we dreamed it all, but my friend still has the handkerchief she bought that day, and that is real enough.

— *Elsie Hill, Eastbourne, Sussex, England*
Jaunary 1978

Lady of the Rock

I was ironing in the living room of our apartment when one of the most startling phenomena of my life occurred. I can only relate this true event as I know it.

I love to iron in the living room where one complete wall is made up of windows and the sun shines bright and cheery, lighting the task. On this summer day in 1951 the radio was playing a popular song and I was humming along with it. Suddenly the music broke off. There was no sound from the radio at all. I wondered if a tube was gone, if the station was having trouble, or whether the electricity was momentarily out. Checking my iron I found the electricity was all right.

It was then I noticed the room had begun to grow dark. Carefully I sat the iron in a safe place and flicked it off. What was happening? Was I about to faint? No. I felt perfectly well. Was there a storm coming, hiding the sun? No. I had been outside just a moment before and the sky was cloudless. What, then, was happening?

The room turned a dark gray color. I backed a few feet away from the ironing board, my eyes adjusting to the peculiar light. There in the center of the room was what appeared to me as a large rock. A feeling of awe came over me and I watched with fascination. My vision seemed glued to the spot.

Then the room radiated with a bluish glow emanating from just above the rock on the floor. In the wink of an eye a woman stood upon the rock.

She was the most beautiful creature I ever have seen. As my eyes traveled from the stone to her bare feet, along the graceful draping of her white and blue dress to the serene features of her face, an enormous sense of peace filled me and I fell to my knees.

"Ave Marie," I said.

She smiled down at me, at the same time extending her hand palm downward, "Dominus Vobiscum," she said.

Again words came from my mouth in Latin, "Et cum spiritu tuo."

A warmth descended upon me, penetrating every fiber of my being. Then the woman and rock were gone, the room returned to its sunny self and the radio was audible, still playing the same song I'd been humming. Everything about me was unchanged.

I picked myself up off my knees and returned to my ironing. My forehead and the palms of my hands were wet with perspiration.

For several days and nights I mulled over the event in silence, afraid to mention it to anyone for fear of being called crazy. The fact that the Lady was trying to tell me something to help me never entered my mind. I was busy wondering why I had used Latin words, whether I was crazy, why did she come to me of all people, etc. True, I had a working knowledge of Latin from the ninth grade and prefixes and suffixes from medical terminology, but I couldn't translate what she had said or what I had said. A quick trip to the library for an English-Latin dictionary satisfied that curiosity. I had said, "Hail Mary," to which recognition she had said, "The Lord be (is) with you," and I had responded correctly, "And thy spirit."

I went to a psychiatrist I had worked for and asked, "Am I crazy?" He laughed and replied, "The very fact you come here and ask me that question makes me answer no. What is your problem?"

I explained.

"Well," he said, "I know things of that nature do occur. If you were a highly religious person I would say your imagination ran away with you. Why it happened — and I'm certain knowing you as I do, that you are not lying about it — I'm not qualified to say. Perhaps some day you will know. Meanwhile, I'll give you some sleeping capsules and you get some rest and forget about it."

But I can never forget my beautiful "Lady of the Rock" or stop my yearning to see her again.

— *Norma Jeffries, San Diego, California*
February 1963

ANGELS SAVED US

"The instant my foot came off the pedal and I looked up to see that speeding car and the terrified woman driving it, I knew my guardian angel was responsible."
— From Richard Bauman's "Bike Angel," page 41

Everyone has a guardian angel who watches over them exclusively, according to Erica Chopich, a Los Angeles-based counselor who says she can see, hear, and talk to angels wherever she goes. We hear from our angels often, she says, but we just don't realize it. Angels are very subtle. Often they will put inspirational ideas in our heads. When we accept their guidance, they're happy.

Sometimes, however, angels won't answer our questions. Chopic said that's because we are all students, here on this Earth to learn. Dealing with tough situations helps us grow — and growth is sometimes painful. If your guardian angel does intervene, as Richard Bauman discovered, the learning process can be a little less painful.

Bike Angel

A guardian angel saved my life one day in 1955, when I was a 13-year-old in a hurry. I was crossing Rosemead Boulevard, a four-lane highway full of fast-moving trucks and cars in South El Monte, California. Traffic lights had been installed at the intersection only a few days earlier.

I had wheeled my bicycle into the crosswalk and was poised to go as soon as the light turned green. At last it changed. I transferred all my weight from my left foot, which had been supporting me on the bike, to my right foot, which was poised on the pedal.

I wanted to push off and crank hard, but it didn't happen that way. My foot came off the pedal. It didn't slip — it was pushed. I lunged forward but the bike didn't move. I cursed under my breath. Then I saw something out of the corner of my eye. I looked to my left and took a short, quick breath. A car was coming — fast.

Though nearly 40 years have passed, I have a crystal-clear memory of that two-tone 1954 Ford with the dark green roof and a pale green body. The chrome bumper, grille, and headlight rings sparkled in the sunlight. The woman driving it had gray, curly hair. Her eyes were open wide and her mouth was agape in horror at what had nearly happened. Her look of terror told me she had seen neither the red light nor me until it was too late.

The instant my foot came off the pedal and I looked up to see that speeding car and the terrified woman driving it, I knew my guardian angel was responsible. That ever-faithful spirit saved me from serious injury and even possible death. My celestial guardian had literally pulled my foot from the pedal. Had I shot into the intersection as I had wanted to, the driver could not have stopped or swerved in time.

Considering the position of the pedal and my momentum, it was almost impossible for my foot to have slipped. My guardian angel saved my life that day, and surely has at other times during my life, but I can't recall any other mortally dangerous times in my life as well as I can that day.

— *Richard Bauman, West Covina, California*
May 1996

Angels in the School Library

In 1973, I was a school librarian in Miami, Florida. One after-noon a siren wailed close by. I raised one of our second-story windows and the clerk, Dot, and I looked into the street below us. An ambulance had stopped and two medics were stooped over a small, crumpled figure lying on the ground behind a school bus.

A group of people crowded around, watching. From the bits of conversation that drifted upward, we gathered that during the lower grade dismissal, the bus had backed into Narcisso, a rambunctious second-grader.

Suddenly Dot exclaimed, "He's dead — I think I heard them say he's dead." She repeated it agitatedly. Feeling devastated, I turned from the window. Suddenly all sound ceased and it was as if I were in another dimension. I gazed around the library in awe. The room had filled with ghostlike beings clothed in gowns of soft white light. One or two of these adult-sized spirits stood close behind each of the 20-some children who were browsing or studying. I knew intuitively that they were guardian angels and that they were dedicated to the boys and girls in their care.

Two third-grade boys approached me in need of assistance. Although I could plainly see their mouths moving, I could not hear a word they were saying. I was in a beautiful mystical space and I wanted to remain there. I knew I was needed, however, so with tremendous effort, I forced myself to concentrate on the boys in front of me. Suddenly, with a jolt, things were back to normal. The spiritual beings disappeared from my sight. The busy hubbub of the library returned and I could hear the boys' requests.

Later, in the school office, I was told that Narcisso had not died. Both of his legs had been broken, but otherwise he was all right. In a few months he was back at school, as lively as ever.

Seeing the guardian angels standing behind the children was a wonderful, uplifting experience. I now believe that we each have an angel or guide to help us along life's way.

— *Carolyn Dignan, Delray Beach, Florida*
September 1996

A Helping Hand

During World War II, I was stationed at Biggs Field, Texas, to take crew training on B-29s. Our flight schooling was proceeding well, without any major problems.

During the first half of our training we were to accomplish a series of high-altitude progressive stalls, done by reducing power while climbing, until the flight controls become sluggish and the airplane starts to shudder. At that point the pilot thrusts the stick forward while increasing power to recover from the stall and then returns the airplane to the desired altitude and speed.

Our airplane and some others had just been modified. The four main gun turrets and the central fire control system had been removed, leaving only the tail turret with guns and radar. This was the combat position. The reduced weight gave the aircraft a faster cruising speed and a slower landing speed and made it capable of higher altitude.

We were assigned a check pilot who was a fighter pilot on his R&R from England. Presumably he had not flown anything larger than a P-47 or P-51. We discovered he had a drinking problem — after we had been flying for several minutes. He had brought a bottle aboard in his flight bag.

I was at my non-combat position as scanner in the aft pressurized section at the right observation blister where I would watch and report landing gear and flap positions. I was also to alert the crew if I saw any problems.

We took off, flying west by northwest, and climbed to our required altitude. We were flying approximately 380 to 400 miles per hour at 35,000 feet. Our pilot was about to begin the first of the series of stalls, which consisted of opening the engine cowl flaps, extending wing flaps for the second stall, and then attempting two more stalls with increased flap positions. The next stall was with the landing gear down, and the last was with the bomb bay doors open. Our speed would be about 170 to 180 miles per hour.

Our pilot did the stalls. But after each stall the drunken check pilot would yell, "That was no — — stall."

Then he yelled, "I'll show you what a — — stall is." Suddenly, he closed everything down at once.

I didn't know what an airplane would do in this condition, but I was about to find out. I felt a cold chill run through me.

The airplane began to shake like a paint mixer and to roll to the right as the nose dropped. Then it got quiet for a while with the nose down and the tail up. It stayed in that position as the wind noise increased. We were no longer flying, but going down like a rock.

In the aft section I could hear the officers yelling at each other: "Pull back on the stick! Run the stabilizer and the trim!"

My curiosity got the better of me so I left my position and propelled myself in the direction I wanted. I felt weightless, and I remember thinking, "This is what Buck Rogers referred to in the comic books." I went back to an instrument panel near the center of the pressure section.

The altimeter showed that we were losing altitude fast and air speed was increasing. I wanted to call the pilot but I had no idea why. I looked at the intercom cord and it was stowed in such a way that it would take too long to release it. Furthermore, I wasn't sure where the switch was. This all went through my mind in a split second.

I found myself swimming back to my seat and looked out the blister as I plugged in my intercom. What I saw made my stomach feel like a bottomless pit: The objects on the ground were getting much too close.

As I squeezed the intercom switch, I said, "Inch the flaps down." Before the last word was out of my mouth I saw the flaps begin to move.

I grabbed the safety belt and pulled myself against the seat and latched it. Then my chin slammed down onto my legs and stayed there for probably a half minute. For a split second I thought, "This may be the end for this crew."

When I was able to lift my head, I looked out and saw only a blur, but the horizon indicated we were flying level. I looked to the rear and saw a long, swirling cloud of dust that our airplane had stirred up off the desert floor. Fortunately there were no hills ahead of us.

As we flew back to Biggs Field, the check pilot begged us not to report him. A few days later I heard he had been reduced in rank from lieutenant colonel to second lieutenant.

As far as I know the airplane was never flown again. The wings were permanently warped, and the wing tips appeared to be at least a foot higher than they should have been.

I had felt as though someone or something had been sitting on my shoulder helping me along and giving me instructions. Lowering the flaps still doesn't seem logical, but I'm sure my helping hand knew more about flying than the crew or I did.

Before that terrifying afternoon, I had never put any stock in the supernatural — but I certainly have since.

— *Dale R. Garbush, Kent, Washington*
February 1997

Heavenly Escort

In 1941 I was a tuberculosis patient at a sanatorium. I had earphones over my head and I was listening to a program of Cole Porter music. It was winter and early evening.

Engrossed in the music I love, I lay there and idly watched a procession of people dressed in white passing my window. They moved slowly, four of them walking in single file while two others supported a third person.

It was getting quite dark and after the procession passed I settled back, humming the tune the orchestra was playing. Suddenly it dawned on me that the people I had seen passing by were not real. I was on the second floor and there were no balconies outside.

I sat up, frightened. A horrible, cold, clammy feeling pressed down on me and I couldn't breathe. Snapping on the light, I rang the bell furiously, but got no answer.

After what seemed like hours I became calm and questioned what I'd seen. I decided I had dozed off for a moment and had dreamed the incident.

The nurse scolded me when she finally came in. Then, seeing how nervous I was, she gave me a sedative.

When I asked her why she was so long coming, she said, "The floor nurses were all busy helping care for the little Mexican girl in room 283. She just died."

I feel I was permitted to witness her "heavenly escort" on her journey home.

— *V. M. Gaither, Wakeeney, Kansas*
June 1955

Saved by My Double

I must have been born with a psychic counterpart or double. At first she was just another child to me but as I grew older and realized there was something odd about her, I began to be afraid.

"You're just imagining things, Weenie," my mother, Vera Williams, said. "You'll outgrow it."

But for another five years I continued to see and be afraid of this "other me." She always appeared without warning. She never said anything but just vanished in a few seconds.

In 1935, when I was 10, we lived on a small rented farm near Gladewater, Texas, then a booming oil town.

"Don't go to the melon patch alone," Mother warned me. Although open to the highway, the patch was hidden from our house by a row of trees and many hobos stopped by to help themselves.

But one hot July day when Mother was busy I decided not to wait until someone could go with me. I ducked behind the chicken house and the barn so Mother wouldn't catch sight of my bright red dress and made my way through the trees.

Heat waves danced on the white sand of the melon patch. Not a bird chirped. Near a clump of sassafras bushes on the far edge of the field I decided I could find some melons growing in the shade. After catching my breath I ran there, wishing that I'd worn my shoes.

I had just picked a melon from the vine when someone said, "Hey, can I buy that melon, little girl?"

A large man in dirty tan clothes was limping towards me with the aid of a walking cane. I didn't stop to think that he must have been hiding in the bushes watching me as I entered the patch alone.

"Oh, you can just have a melon," I said politely.

"Now that wouldn't be right," he replied, coming closer. He reached into his pocket and pulled out a piece of change. "Here now, take this."

"No, sir," I said as he pushed it at me. "I can't." I started backing away from him. "You'll have to see my Daddy!"

He began to curse and shoved the money back into his pocket. Then I realized with horror that he was exposing himself.

As I stood petrified with fear he raised the big walking cane above my head. He was going to hit me!

Suddenly a little voice cried, "Run, Weenie, run!" Behind the man I saw a little girl in a bright red dress and with yellow hair — my double. The man whirled as if he had heard something too. The walking stick came down but because he had glanced back it missed me.

I didn't take time to think or scream. As he raised the cane to strike again, I ran. My feet flew, dodging melons and ripping through vines. I'd almost reached the row of trees when I stubbed my bare toe. I fell, sprawling headlong on the ground.

I scrambled to my hands and knees but when I glanced back I saw a strange scene. The man had stopped running after me and was lashing out with his cane as if he'd caught someone. As I gasped for breath he suddenly whirled and with giant hopping strides ran back into the sassafras thicket.

Once on my feet I never stopped running or screaming till I reached the house. Mother made out enough from my incoherent sobs to know that someone had tried to attack me.

We had no telephone or close neighbors so when she saw I was all right, we waited until my stepfather Lonnie Williams came home from town.

Father went to the field and found the footprints and indentations from the cane that confirmed my story but of course the stranger had fled.

I did not see my double again until 10 years later. One night as I returned home from visiting my mother in the hospital I snapped on my bedroom light. There, sitting on the side of my bed, was my double. She was grown now too. As always she was dressed just like me. Her hands were resting on her lap and on her finger was a double of my class ring. As I stared at her, she vanished. I've never seen her again.

— Florence Sypert, Longview, Texas
August 1975

The Children

More than a decade ago, on Rice Lake, in the Kawartha Lakes region of Canada, something happened to me that has always haunted me. It was a sunny day — clear sky, green grass, blue water, a perfect vacation day in the trailer park. Two young kids, alone, tried to board a little boat from a dock overlooking deep water. Somehow, one or the other of the children must have rocked the boat and sent them both into the lake. They both drowned.

It was about 5:00 P.M. that same day, and I think just about everybody had heard of the tragedy — everyone but me, that is. The sun was low in the sky and I figured there was almost two hours left to do some fishing. So I took my small boat out on the lake, about a 20-minute run. As it became darker, I tried to make my way back, but the bottom of the outboard motor hit a log or something and smashed the gearbox in half with a terrible shock.

I was stranded in the middle of the lake, and I had stupidly brought only one oar. It was a long, heavy, rowing oar, practically useless by itself. I tried rowing with the bulky thing but could make little distance. It was almost dark, and no other boats were in sight. Darkness! You cannot believe the utter blackness of a country night. The only lights in the sky were the stars, the full moon, and the planet Jupiter. I could only see about 20 feet, and only make out vague shadows in the water (like thick, black oil). An intermittent breeze, rather than my own efforts, had taken my boat into an area covered with many thousands of reeds and bulrushes, most standing four or five feet high. I knew where I was; I knew about those damn reeds. The area is an intricate maze of waterways. Now I really could get lost. I kept struggling to stay outside of them, but it was useless. A current caused by streams running into the swamps held the boat in the reeds and pulled me in. I was helpless, at least until I reached a calmer area.

Confused and exhausted, I tied the boat to a clump of reeds. The temperature became very cold. Sitting there quietly, I noticed, for the first time, a whiny whistling or singing sound that the reeds were making, and, between the puffs of wind that made them sing, a sound like breathing or gasping. Perhaps it was just that I was sitting there alone in the absolute dark, but my hearing seemed amplified.

Then I heard, rising from the water, the sounds of a couple of children laughing or giggling and sometimes whispering, as if telling secrets to each other. About 10 yards ahead of me, I heard them, but I saw nothing. Thinking I must be near land, I called out to them, but I heard no answer. Instead, an instant silence lasting several seconds descended (even the reeds stayed silent). Then the breeze came up and I heard it again — the reeds and that laughing. I got up and yelled. I grabbed the oar and began banging it against the boat. I still heard nothing and the same silence as before remained. Soon the laughter began again and I decided to find the source. Surely the children were there. I took the oar and pushed the boat along the reed beds toward the sounds.

After an hour or so, with the children seemingly always just ahead of me, I came to a place where I could see a few lights from my trailer camp. All the sounds now faded away. I was back home in familiar territory and everything returned to normal.

— *David N. Law, Scarborough, Ontario, Canada*
April 1995

Something Pushed Me

My story begins years ago, in the fall of 1929, when Los Angeles was on the verge of a financial crisis. Business, however, went on as usual but loan companies refused to extend the time of payment on second mortgages, or increase first mortgages on residential property.

At that time my home had two mortgages — the second a trust deed for about $2,500, which was due in less than a month. All my efforts to renew it or increase the first mortgage failed.

The loss of any home is a disaster to those concerned. But I was the sole support of myself and a teenage daughter. I earned just enough to pay our living expenses, taxes, and monthly house payments, and so had cause for worry.

Fortunately, shortly before the scheduled foreclosure proceedings were to begin, a friend who had sold some property in another state offered to lend me the money to pay off the second mortgage on my home and trust me for the necessary security. He gave me his personal check on an out-of-state bank.

The next day I went downtown to deposit his check in a bank considered the soundest financial institution in town. The president, a highly respected citizen, had a fine reputation as a trustworthy and shrewd business man and the bank building itself was splendid, inside and outside.

When I entered the bank a man in an expensive uniform helped me locate the clerk in charge of new accounts. Then I stood for some time behind a long line of depositors who also were opening new accounts.

Finally, I was first in line and I told the clerk that I wanted to open a new account. He asked for my name and address, filled out the deposit slip, then gave it back to me with a pen so I could endorse my check for $2,500.

There were 10 people behind me waiting impatiently for an opportunity to open new accounts. I took the pen and had begun to write my first name when something pushed me away from the clerk's window — pushed me so hard I almost lost my balance.

Frightened, I dropped the pen, picked up my check and ran swiftly from the bank while everyone in the building stared at me as if I suddenly had lost my mind.

Once outside, I breathed deeply and didn't care what anyone thought about my flight. Then I went directly to the loan company and endorsed my check as suggested and made arrangements to give my friend the proper security.

A week or so later, Los Angeles newspapers carried big headlines announcing that the president of the bank from which I bad fled had shot himself because of unwise investments and mismanagement. It was the stock market crash of 1929.

The bank closed its doors and never reopened them. Depositors lost hundreds of thousands of dollars. Their checks bounced everywhere. But my home was safe, thanks to my invisible friend who pushed me away from the new accounts window.

— *Clara R. Lain, Burbank, California*
March 1966

REMARKABLE RECOVERIES

*But as he lay dying, Dad called me over to his bedside and said,
"Darlene, Earl doesn't have cancer anymore. This is my gift to
you."*

— From Darlene Harris' "A Life for a Soul," page 55

Remarkable recoveries would be easy to dismiss as wishful thinking and coincidence — were it not for the medical reports. In
countless cases, doctors have given up hope and prepared families for the worst just before their patients make a complete turn-
around. The details are corroborated by objective evidence and
independent witnesses, including medical records and the acccounts
of resuers, paramedics, police, and physicians. Whether the means to
the cure involves healing by faith, touch, or psychic powers, the stories defy conventional explanations.

A Life for a Soul

As my father lay in an emergency room, he drifted in and out of sleep. When he was awake, he riddled us with strange questions. Who, he asked, was the man in the corner? We assured my dad that no one was there — but we knew in our hearts that it was the angel of death waiting to take my daddy's soul. He asked us about a flight of steps he could see — but he was half blind and the curtains were pulled around his bed. All through the night, he would wake up, ask a question, and fall back asleep. He once woke up and asked us to turn out the bright lights over his head. He said they were hurting his eyes. We turned out the overhead lights, and he went back to sleep. He woke again and said, "I thought I told you to turn out those bright lights. They hurt my eyes." We knew in our hearts that it was the white light of Christ that he was seeing.

Dad had always been fond of my husband Earl. Sadly, Earl was fighting cancer at the time. But as he lay dying, Dad called me over to his bedside and said, "Darlene, Earl doesn't have cancer anymore. This is my gift to you." I tried to explain to him that my husband's cancer was in remission, but he still did indeed have cancer. Dad yelled loudly at me, "Darlene, you better believe what I say to you. Take him to three of the best cancer doctors, and they will all tell you that his cancer is gone."

I thought no more of what my dad had said on his deathbed until a couple of months later. My husband picked me up from work, and he had a puzzled look on his face. I asked him why, and he said that his doctor had told him that he didn't have to come back anymore. The doctor told him he was fine.

My great-grandmother once told me that when the angel of death takes a soul, he also gives a life back in return. I cannot have children, so I feel God decided to give me my husband's life in return for my father's soul. I never gave much thought to the spirit world, but God and my father sure made a believer out of me.

— Darlene Harris, Brooksville, Florida
March 1997

Healed with the Hand
of a Fresh-Dead Man

C an mind triumph over matter? Some people maintain that it can, and go so far as to insist that the triumph is the basis of so-called "magic" and of miracle cures such as those that occur at Lourdes.

If this contention is correct, I wonder wherein certain of my personal experiences fit. I wonder, too, whether an ability to "see ghosts" — I am sure that it is an ability because some people cannot see a ghost that is perfectly visible to others — is an individual matter or whether it is inherent in certain families.

My mother saw three different ghosts during her lifetime. Her brother saw two more. Her younger sister, who was the seventh child of a seventh child, beheld a terrifying apparition that she would rarely discuss.

As a child I lived with my parents in the sleepy little village of Headley, Surrey, in the south of England. It possessed but one small general store, kept by a Mrs. Barcock, a quaint, silver-haired old soul who possessed an encyclopedic knowledge of herb-cures, folklore, and country superstitions. Her ability to diagnose the complaints of sick animals, from pedigreed bulls to pet canaries, was known for miles around. All the farmers and breeders in the neighborhood consulted her. No veterinary surgeon could have made a living in the district!

Annie Barcock also possessed "second sight." I can remember hearing her say with great certainty that the *Titanic* would sink with great loss of life before it reached New York. And when the "Agadir Incident" was at its height she said that war would break out between Britain and Germany in August 1914, and that, before peace was signed, the czars of Russia would be no more.

In April 1914, when I was 12, I developed a most disfiguring goiter — if it was a goiter. Dr. Lithgow Braidwood of Chichester finally referred my parents to Dr. Frank Kidd, an American surgeon who was working with a research team at Guy's Hospital in London. Doctor Braidwood's suspicions were confirmed. The "goiter" was malignant and so situated that it was separated from the jugular vein by only a tiny fraction of an inch. An operation (in those days) was too risky to be justified. All this, of course, was spoken only in whispers to prevent my finding out. But children do find things out for themselves and I was not in ignorance for long.

On the Sunday afternoon following the visit to Dr. Kidd, my father took me for a drive. Part of the routine on such occasions was to call at Mrs. Barcock's for a glass of her home-brewed ginger beer on the way home. She knew that a specialist had been consulted and she was all agog to know what he had said.

"Ah, sir," she said after a whispered conference with my father. "Don't 'ee b'live one word of 'un. I can tell 'ee the one an' only sartin cure for him. If so be, that is, as the young gen'leman do have the courage to take it."

My father, who had a great respect for the old crone's knowledge of "cures and simples," asked her what it was, perhaps expecting her to say that my "goiter" should be whipped with stinging nettles, or some such thing.

"He maun stroke it with the hand of a fresh dead man, sir. Once to and once fro. But he maun do it himself and he maun be alone with the corpse."

My father was very, very angry with her for saying such a thing in my hearing. Both he and my mother were certain that I would suffer from nightmares for months to come! In order to take my mind off the subject by a change of scenery, I was whisked off to the seaside two days later, where my mother and I stayed at a hideously genteel private hotel.

I have often wondered why I had such utter, implicit faith in old Mother Barcock. I was determined somehow to get access to the corpse of a dead man but I was under no illusions as to the difficulty of doing so. Dead bodies are not easy for a 12-year-old boy to come by. I knew from Sherlock Holmes stories that dead bodies were kept in cold-storage in hospitals and I worked out several schemes to get into a mortuary, only to abandon them as impractical. Yet, I knew that I soon must get access to the body of a "fresh dead man," as I had heard one hotel servant inform another that I had only a few months to live.

Is there indeed some destiny that shapes our ends? Be that as it may, the improbable happened. The hotel's star boarder, a crochety old gentleman with chronic heart disease, died suddenly in his bed when a chambermaid woke him up with a tray of early tea. She screamed the news hysterically and I heard every word.

Sick and clammy with a mixture of fear and excitement, I ran along the passage to his room. I could hear feet clumping up the stairs and I knew I had only seconds in which to act. I still can see the fat old man hanging over the side of his bed, his face purple and his false teeth, having fallen out of his mouth, lodged in the front of his nightshirt. I grabbed his hand and rubbed his fingers to and fro, once each way, over my disfigured neck. I can remember whispering, "Please, God, let it work." Then I must have fainted.

We returned borne by the first available train, my mother completely panic-stricken. The only comment I can recollect my father making at the time was that "he'd like to wring that so-and-so old witch's neck for her." Just before my bedtime Mother remembered about the nightmares I was expected to have. She thought that maybe Dr. Braidwood had better call and give me a sleeping draught. Dr. Braidwood apparently did not think that I was in need of any powerful sedative. But he left a couple of tablets in case I woke up during the night.

For some reason I was not supposed to know he had been sent for, but I met him in the hall just as he was going. Catching sight of me, he exclaimed, "Good God, Boy! " and led me to the better light of the open doorway. The extraordinary look on his face really did frighten me for a moment as his fingers explored the growth. But when he smiled at my parents I knew everything was all right, and my heart began to race.

"This is quite unbelievable," he said quietly. "Look for yourself ... it has shrunk by almost one third." By the Wednesday morning the goiter, tumor, or whatever it was, had disappeared completely.

Now, what cured me? Was it my faith in old Mother Barcock's folklore? Or did she, who certainly would have been burned as a witch in the not-so-very-distant past, really "know something?"

— *Major Francis Martin-Stuart*
May 1963

The Disappearing Warts

In the summer of 1918, when I was 10 years old, ugly warts suddenly appeared on my left hand. I felt guilty; Mother often had warned me not to play with toads and I had disobeyed her. I felt God was punishing me for disobeying Mother's dictum.

In September at the beginning of the school term all of us had to undergo a physical examination. Noticing the many warts on my hand the examiner ordered me to have them removed. I didn't know what dire consequences awaited me but I had to tell my mother that the warts must be removed. Rather coldbloodedly, I thought, she said, "The warts will have to be cut out, one by one, or burned out with acid. Take your choice."

Word of my predicament quickly spread through the old Brooklyn tenement in which we lived. One old granny, Mrs. Feldman, came down to tell Mother she could get rid of my warts. She said she had an Old-World remedy: "Let me have a thin white string about 30 inches long and a lighted candle." When mother produced these, Granny Feldman sat me down on a kitchen chair, then asked Mother to leave the room — which she did, reluctantly.

Granny peered intently at my left hand and mumbled something unintelligible, meanwhile looping the white thread into knots. When she finally knotted the entire length of thread she held it above the candle flame, which burned it quickly. Putting her finger to her lips, Granny forbade me to speak as she left the kitchen. I laughed at her, forgetting to say thank you.

Mother returned and I told her about the knotting and burning of the white thread. She smiled. "White magic, not black magic — but you can't tell ...."

That night I dreamed I was choking. In a cold sweat I struggled awake, jumped out of bed and turned on the light. Something made me connect the dream with Granny Feldman's visit and I looked at my left hand. It was perfectly smooth; not a wart remained.

To this day, 50 years later, they have not come back.

— *Sol Harris Goldstein, Brooklyn, New York*
August 1969

Don't Worry

I was born on September 13, 1949, without hope of survival. Low birthweight babies had a more difficult time then, typically surviving only a few weeks or months. My mother was six months pregnant when I was born and I weighed only one pound, seven ounces. When I was older, she told me she could have held me in the palm of her hand when I was born.

The medical professionals were not encouraged, and told her that no baby that weighed so little at birth had ever survived at their hospital.

One morning, my mother was lying in bed at the hospital, depressed and worried. She didn't want to believe the doctors and nurses. Then, two men sat down on the edge of the bed. One was her father. The other, a handsome man whom she had seen only in photographs, she recognized as her father-in-law.

Both men, however, had been dead for some time. Her father died two years before I was born, and her father-in-law died when my father was 10.

She told me she wasn't afraid. "I was surrounded by a peaceful feeling. Something I couldn't explain."

My grandfathers told her, "Don't worry or listen to your doctors — they are wrong. Your daughter will survive and grow up to be a wonderful daughter and a beautiful child."

The doctors and nurses noticed a change in her attitude and thought she wasn't facing facts. They explained that the odds were a million to one that I would survive, and if I did, I would have many health problems. They even told her to pray that I would die so I wouldn't suffer.

My mother smiled and kept her positive attitude. I kept fighting and the doctors shook their heads in amazement. Mother left the hospital but came back every day to stare at me through the glass wall. In those days, patients weren't allowed to hold a premature baby or enter the premature section of the nursery.

I gained weight slowly. The tubes were removed, one by one, and I began to look like a normal baby. On Christmas Day, after more than three months in the hospital, she brought me home. I weighed five pounds. My grandfathers delivered a message, and my mother believed them.

> — *Nancy Duci Denofio, Glenville, New York*
> *February 1994*

The Healer's Helper

When I was 11 years old and attending the Lincoln School in Detroit, Michigan, an incident happened that was so supernatural that it is still vivid in my memory.

I'd had a running ulcer on the back of my right hand for a long time, and it wasn't getting any better. No matter what home-prescribed medicines Mother applied to the ulcer, it refused to get any better.

Finally the ulcer began to pain me so terribly that my mother took me to see a doctor.

The doctor didn't even know what it was. She took me to another doctor, but this one, too, said that it was an unknown ulcer and that he could do nothing for it. Mom took me to more doctors and to several hospitals, all to no avail.

Was it cancer? Several doctors thought so. But, of course, in those days no one knew exactly what cancer was.

Then one day as I was coming home from school, a shabbily dressed old man stopped me on the street and said, "Son, I'm the Healer's Helper. You have a terrible sore on your right hand. The doctors can't do anything for it. No one can do anything for it — no one, that is, except me. I was sent to cure it for you."

As if in a hypnotic trance, I put out my hand.

The strange old man who said he was the Healer's Helper spat in the palm of his own hand and rubbed it on my ulcer.

"Go on home, son, and don't wash your hand for three days and three nights," he said. Then he turned and disappeared around a street corner.

Still in somewhat of a hypnotic state, I went home and told Mother about the incident. She was dubious but was willing to try anything if it would ease the constant pain in my hand. So for three days and three nights I didn't wash my hand and gradually, as those three days passed, the pain decreased, and the ulcer began to dry up. On the fourth day when I finally washed the hand, the ulcer was healed. I never saw the man again.

> — *Frank Love as told to Bob L. Austin, Jackson, Michigan*
> *September 1959*

A Cure Freely Given

Twenty-two years ago we were living deep in the North Carolina mountains, miles from Banner Elk, when Sue, our two-year-old, had thrush, a disease characterized by big, ugly blisters in the mouth. Having neither phone nor car, I carried her to a neighbor's house for help.

"We'll take her to John C.," Lola Wright said. "He's a seventh son of a seventh son who never saw his father and he'll cure her."

"That's the silliest thing I ever heard," I exploded. "It's ignorant superstition."

"I know he can do it," Lola insisted, "and if Sue isn't well in the morning, we'll get to town somehow."

"All right," I said, impressed by her seriousness. "I'll try anything if there's a chance it will help her in a hurry. But I still don't believe it."

The man was haying in a field above his home the next morning, and we carried Sue to his wagon. She liked him at once and was perfectly quiet when he picked her up, put her on his knee, covered her mouth with his and blew three times. Then, with a few kind words, he put her down and stood up, ready to return to his work.

"Is that all you're going to do?" I asked, amazed. "Yes," he said. "The blisters will be gone by evening and she'll be well."

"What do I owe you?" I asked.

"Nothing," he answered. "It's a gift freely given to me and I can't accept anything for it."

Sue stopped fretting on the way home. By evening, not a blister was to be seen in her mouth. Never since that experience have I labeled things outside my knowledge "ignorant superstition."

— *Helen Mahon, Casper, Wyoming*
March 1960

The Image on the Shade

I was the third child of very poor parents and was completely unwanted. My mother did not want another child and, above all, not another boy. To make matters worse, I was a mute.

My grandmother, Mrs. Amy Letts, was the only person who showed any love for me. She would sit hour after hour, trying to teach me to say one word. In January 1930, when I was almost five years old, she died. I didn't know what death was, but I did know that I missed her very much.

One night as I lay in bed, not sleeping but just staring at the window shade, I saw a light appear on it. Then the head and shoulders of my grandmother took shape. She was in profile, but she turned and smiled at me. Then she put her fingers to her lips.

I shook my older brother, who shared my bed. He looked up sleepily and said, "That's a picture of Grandma," and turned over to return to sleep. Just then there was a sensation in my throat as if a rubber band snapped and I woke everyone in the household by screaming for my grandmother.

When the lights were turned on, the image disappeared. Everyone except my brother thought that I had dreamed it. From that time on, I could talk, although I stuttered for years. Now, at 31, my voice is perfectly normal.

— *Jerry William Carmelle, Chicago, Illinois*
December 1957

ORACLES AND FORTUNETELLERS

I sat looking into the flickering candle flames. Suddenly a picture formed! I saw Cynthia in complete bridal attire — but she didn't even have a steady boyfriend!
— From Helen Seaton's "The Bayberry Candles," page 69

In addition to prophetic dreams and precognitive visions, we often receive psychic messages from outside sources. Gypsies, psychics, and fortunetellers can give us accurate predictions, messages from the spirit world, and unusual but effective solutions. Ouija boards are another common means of communicating with spirits, learning the future, or gaining otherwordly advice. Psychometry allows some individuals to learn information about an object merely by coming into contact with it. And as long as we've been building fires, images have appeared in the smoke and flames, such as the futures Helen Seaton witnessed when she watched her burning candles.

"Cross My Palm with Silver"

I can't tell you why I decided to take a walk along the river that cold October 24, 1960. I had an incurable heart condition and over-fatigue, exercise, or chilling winds leave me weak and breathless. Yet in the middle of my quiet breakfast, I put down the cup of hot coffee, threw on an old coat and woolen scarf, and hurried over the bank to walk on the cold windy shore.

As I trotted along, I looked back over the bank and saw the smoke rising from my neighbor's chimney. It gave me some comfort for I was a little disturbed at this queer thing I felt compelled to do.

Only an instant was my gaze withdrawn from my path, yet when I turned again, there directly in front of me stood a gypsy. Where she came from or how she got there so quickly, I'll never know. She was completely alone.

She reached out two soiled hands, palms up, in a pleading gesture. "Please, do not be alarmed, I had to come ... you must know the truth. Will you let me tell your fortune?"

I was angry. I don't believe in such things. And I was a little frightened too. Was this gypsy really here, or had I taxed my strength beyond reason? I looked back quickly toward home and there was John, my husband, at the gate. I waved and he waved back. She's real, I decided, and my courage returned. I knew John would wait for me.

I turned back to the gypsy. "I don't want my fortune told," I said. "I'm busy and in a hurry." Her dark eyes pleaded. "Please. I had to come to you. Don't you understand? You must know the truth! Come ...cross my palm with silver. Please, so I can tell you quickly. I must hurry."

I realized my hand already had laid hold on a piece of silver in my pocket. Slowly I drew it out. No harm, I thought, John is waiting. It might even be interesting. I crossed the gypsy's palm with silver.

With my hand between her two cold palms, I bent close to hear. Her voice was low as she said, "Someone, whom you think is a friend, in your neighborhood, has put a curse on you. It is ruining your health, your heart. You must break this spell. Tomorrow at exactly noon, lock your door and sit down. Then slowly drink a large glass of water, drink it down in one large breath. There will be an interruption, but do not stop. Finish the water and keep your eyes closed.

"Do this again the second day when again there will be an interruption. On the third day, as you drink, this person will come rushing to you to borrow something, but finish your water. Drink it down and then answer the door, but refuse whatever she asks. Turn her away. At once the spell will then be broken."

The gypsy turned without another word and disappeared. I hurried home.

John met me. "What are you doing?" he asked. "Trying to die young? It's cold, dear. Let's get into the house. Who is your friend?"

I told John everything and he only laughed. Yet I knew, no matter how little of this I believed, I never would be satisfied unless I carried out the gypsy's instructions. The next day at exactly noon I locked the door and sat down. I took a deep breath and began to drink the water. At once the phone began to ring, loud and insistent in my quiet house. But I finished the water and the ringing ceased.

It was the same on the second day.

On the third day I must confess that my hands shook so I could hardly hold the glass but I finished the last drop of water.

Suddenly someone was coming in at the gate, running swiftly up the walk, onto the porch. There was a frantic knocking at the door. Cold chills seized me as I opened the door just a foot's width.

There stood my next-door neighbor. She was breathless and seemed confused and embarrassed. "I'm sending a package overseas and for the life of me I cannot find any wrapping cord. Do you have a piece handy? About two yards will do. "

"No," I said very firmly, "I have no wrapping cord to loan you and I'm busy." I closed the door. We were not friends after that.

During the next week I made my regular visit to the doctor. He was so amazed he called in two other doctors for consultation. My "incurable" heart condition had vanished and has not returned. I don't know what to think! How do you account for it?

— *Velma Sinclair, Wheeling, West Virginia*
April 1965

The Bayberry Candles

As Christmas 1967 approached, my younger daughter Sandra Mateika came upon a box of two olive-green candles in a gift shop. Tucked in the box was a slip of paper relating that these were bayberry candles and that if one burned them between Christmas and New Year's Eve and made a wish, the wish would come true. The idea intrigued me and Cynthia bought them.

On Christmas Eve the whole family gathered at Sandra's home in Ladd, Illinois, to exchange gifts and have a party. We distributed the presents and the last package, attractively wrapped and tied, contained my little bayberry candles.

I couldn't wait to light them and make a wish. I sat before the candles, staring into the flames and thinking how nice it would be if my wish did come true.

I have a large family: My sons William, still in the Air Force, and Jerry working in Waukesha, Wisconsin, my daughter Sandra and her husband Frank (who were giving the party) and my daughter Cynthia who lived at home with me. I loved them all dearly but I'd been harboring a wish to spend a week or two alone, somewhere away from family responsibilities.

This was my wish as I sat looking into the flickering candle flames. Suddenly a picture formed! I saw Cynthia in complete bridal attire — but she didn't even have a steady boyfriend!

I couldn't tear my eyes from the candles. Next I saw my oldest daughter holding a tiny baby in her arms but I knew she wasn't expecting a child. Finally I saw myself walking with the aid of crutches!

I forced myself to stand up. Sandra looked concerned as she said, "Mother, your face is absolutely white!"

I drew her aside and told her what I had seen in the flames. I knew she would tell her brothers and sister about my "vision," for they always teased me about my superstitions and my interest in the occult.

But my wish did come true! The next summer I traveled alone to Wisconsin Dells for a vacation. In nearby Waukesha I attended an art show and, watching the outdoor exhibits rather than my path, I tripped and broke my ankle. For a time I had to use crutches.

By that time, however, Cynthia had met a wonderful young man, Ralph Krogulski of Peru, Illinois, and they were married in December 1968. And Sandra and Frank adopted a four-day-old son! When I went to see him for the first time she was holding him in the bend of her arm, precisely as I pictured them in the flickering flames of the bayberry candles.

— *Helen Seaton, Oglesby, Illinois*
July 1970

A Mother's Touch

My mother was psychic and was especially gifted in psychometry. At dinner parties she amazed and amused our friends by holding various objects of theirs and giving detailed descriptions of where a particular object came from, events associated with it, and so on. I thought it a clever and baffling sort of parlor game.

Several years prior to her death in April 1936, I decided to test her power myself. I had just the object, a button from the uniform of a soldier who had seen some of the bloodiest action in World War I. Mother had not seen this button in years. I knew it would be as far from her mind as anything I could think of.

I wrapped the button in several handkerchiefs to conceal its shape. Mother could not have known whether it was a ring or any one of dozens of small objects. I regretted what I had done the instant Mother took the wrapped button in her hands. She was horrified. She described a scene of battle that made my hair stand on end — men dying, guns roaring, planes diving, all the confusion and terror of war. She threw the small bundle clear across the room. I felt a little ashamed that I needed that experience to be convinced of her great gift.

— *Delores Simi, Prescott, Arizona*
November 1956

The Ouija Prediction

I often have played with the Ouija board and had a lot of fun getting answers. One day, however, it wasn't quite so much fun. A friend of mine, John Cotrell, was asking some questions. He had been offered a choice of positions and was wondering which one he should accept.

"Would you help me with the Ouija board?" he asked. We always had had great success working it together and we made arrangements to try it that evening.

The board was quite active when we started but we quickly found that any time we asked a question concerning Johnny or his work we always received the same answer: "dead" or "will die." John had a patient who was dying and we thought it concerned this patient, but were rather disgusted because we couldn't get any other answers. We tried all sorts of questions but the answer was the same, "dead" or "will die."

Suddenly I looked at Johnny and he was beginning to look haunted, so I suggested we stop this nonsense. This was July 10, 1955.

A week later we had dinner together at the Strata Room and watched the planes coming and going. "There is nothing I would rather do than spend the rest of my life flying," Johnny said, looking wistfully at the soaring planes.

"Have you decided which job you are going to take?" I asked. I knew he had to decide shortly or lose both opportunities.

"Somehow, it doesn't seem important anymore," he said.

"Not important?" I exclaimed, shocked. "Why, Johnny?"

"I don't know why," he replied with a smile. "It just seems unnecessary for me to make up my mind about it."

"Perhaps the answer will come," I said, knowing that he believed in guidance.

"It would be wonderful, flying around in those beautiful clouds," he said, changing the subject.

I let the matter drop. The very next Sunday, John was invited to fly with an outstanding captain, John Gaines, in a small plane. They had been up for about one-half hour when suddenly, on the clear blue day of July 4, 1955, the plane was caught in a downdraft and crashed into the nearby foothills. Both men were killed instantly.

The Ouija board was right when it predicted "dead" or "will die" to all John's questions. And I believe Johnny knew it meant him and that is why be ceased to worry about a job decision. The Ouija board had told him.

— *Val Spires, Boise, Idaho*
February 1963

The Gypsy and the Scapecat

As far back as I can remember, my mother has detested the idea of owning a pet, especially a cat. It was hard to understand her excuse for not liking cats — the mess they make — since she was not so adept at keeping house herself. One day she finally disclosed the truth about why she would never consider owning even a friendly feline.

In the spring of 1943, in the Greek village of Petalidi, a gypsy knocked at the door of my mother's home. The gypsy asked my grandmother, "Do you recall the branch of oleander someone placed on your doorstep on May first?"

"Yes, it was only a joke," grandmother replied.

"You are wrong, madam," the gypsy said. "It was witchcraft."

The gypsy begged my grandmother to let her enter the house to remove the hex from grandmother and the family. My grandmother told the gypsy she did not believe in witchcraft, and that she was a widow with four children to raise.

The gypsy insisted, "Yes, I know, madam. First your husband died, then his death was followed by your newborn son's crib death, and now your oldest son, Jim, is suffering from intense pain in his right arm that the doctors can't diagnose. Please allow me to remove the hex from you and your family. It is fatal."

My grandmother led her into the kitchen. There stood my mother and her three siblings, silent, their eyes fixed on the visitor.

The gypsy asked for a glass of water. She placed a cloth over it and chanted in her gypsy tongue. After a few moments, she removed the cloth from the glass. The water had turned to seawater. It appeared cloudy with sand accumulating at the bottom of the glass. She then pulled a fishhook out of the glass. Attached to the hook were bits of cloth, buttons, a tiny fish, and a few strands of hair. The gypsy said that these were personal items that the original caster of the spell had stolen from the family. The household cat was in the kitchen at that moment, and the gypsy poured the water from the glass over the animal.

Next, the gypsy asked my grandmother for a round loaf of bread. She cut a circle out of the middle of the bread, and placed the fishhook with all the personal articles used in the spell inside the bread. The gypsy said that at midnight she would go out to the shore to toss the piece of bread — with the magic — into the sea. Then, the gypsy said, a hen would come out of the sea with her chicks, and she would feed them the remainder of the bread.

The gypsy warned my grandmother never to buy herself a cat again because it would die. She had thrown the hex off the family and onto the cat forever. Coincidentally, whatever killed the cat lifted the pain out of my uncle Jim's arm.

Years later, when he was in his thirties, my uncle Jim tried owning a cat. Unfortunately, the cat died when it arrived at its new home. This incident perpetuated the fear in my mother and her siblings: Any cat that they brought home would die.

— Venetia Kapp, Brooklyn, New York
November 1996

The Face in the Smoke

One morning when I was a young girl living in my mother's house in San Francisco, I was packing a small suitcase, preparing to visit my cousins across the Bay in Alameda. While thus occupied I noticed small gusts of smoke issuing from the carpeted floor. Yet there was no smell of smoke. I touched the carpet in spots.

There was no heat and certainly no fire. Then I examined everything, even turned out the scrap basket for fear a lighted cigarette had been tossed there.

I opened the door leading into the passage, searched that particular floor carefully, leaned over the staircase, and looked down. Still I could find no sign or smell of a fire, so I returned to my room and went on with my packing, thinking it was all my imagination.

But it was not. The minute I closed the door and was alone, the little smoke puffs got busy as elves. As I watched, the smoke gradually formed into a cylinder about the circumference of my forearm, slowly rose, growing darker as it did so, and moved toward a vacant place on the wall. There it turned and twisted before my astonished eyes until it became a perfect oval picture frame, and in that frame developed the face of the most attractive man I had ever imagined. He was a young man, completely unknown to me. It was like the Technicolor films of today — he was as alive as actors on the screen. I noted the deep, sea-blue eyes, the noble forehead, generous mouth, a chin strong but not aggressively so, the hair, light brown and carefully brushed.

As I gazed spellbound, his face broke into the most delightful smile imaginable. Before I could return the smile, both the frame and the face had vanished.

Now at this period of my life I was about to accept the proposal of a San Francisco banker who, with the hope that I would occupy it, had built a home on the peak of Belvedere. He was a very fine man but 30 years my senior. I wasn't in love with anyone else and had decided to accept him until the time of my vision.

On the ferry on my way to the party, the unknown man of my vision haunted me. I felt I could never find him — perhaps he did not even exist.

Arriving at my destination, I gave my suitcase to the Chinese boy who opened the door and went directly into the living room where perhaps a dozen people had gathered. In the midst of greeting my cousins I suddenly froze, for there, chatting easily with those surrounding him, was the man of my vision, speaking in a deep voice that stirred me to the depths.

In three days we were engaged. We married and lived happily. For from that first morning when I saw his face on the wall of the

San Francisco house until the day he lay in death in his ancestral home in Greenwich, Washington County, New York, I never got tired of looking at it.

To conclude, he had never heard of me and had never heard my name, so in this case mental telepathy seems definitely excluded.

— *Mrs. Allan McLane Mowry, New York, New York*
March 1951

The Ouija Board Is Not a Toy

World War II was raging in Europe when my friend Romesa asked me to store a few things for her while she followed her husband to his new post. "Use what you like," she said. Among the things she left with me was a very old, beautifully hand-crafted Ouija board. Her father had brought it from India when he came to America.

My husband, Tom, had been burned in an accident at the 36th Street Air Force Base in Miami, Florida, and had just been released from the hospital to convalesce at our apartment. After a couple of days, both of us were looking for entertainment. It was then that I recalled Romesa's Ouija board stored in the hall closet.

Uppermost in our thoughts at the time was the uncertainty over Tom's next transfer. His regiment was expected to ship out either to Europe or Japan, so we asked the Ouija board when Tom would have to go. It spelled out "White as snow."

"What is white as snow?" we asked.

"Sand," it answered, and the little iron-shaped guide ran off the board. Although we tried for quite a while to get a clearer statement from the board, it apparently had no more to say. We were very dissatisfied with its peculiar, mystifying message anyway, so I put the Ouija board back among Romesa's things and forgot about it.

Over the next year, I followed Tom to several bases within the States. While in Alamogordo, New Mexico, I returned to our apartment one day, and found a little pile of what appeared to be snow by the front steps. The weather was hot and snow would surely melt, so I bent down to feel it. I was shocked to find it was sand — chalk-white sand. When I asked the landlady about it, she said a neighbor had brought it back from the White Sands National Monument, which is only twenty miles from Alamogordo. A year later the area became famous for the atom bomb testing grounds, but at the time we didn't know such a place existed. A week later Tom was transferred again.

— *Mildred Stamos, Seymour, Tennessee*
October 1989

The Dancing Candle

Martha Ann Slemons and I live in neighboring apartments in Philadelphia and have been close friends for many years. For some time we have held regular séances with the Ouija board, usually by candlelight. A number of evidential messages have come through from entities purporting to be deceased relatives or friends.

Starting in the summer of 1968, however, the Ouija board sessions took a strange turn. A persistent spirit, who identified herself as "Hettie," monopolized the board and blocked access to any other discarnate who might have been inclined to communicate.

Either Hettie couldn't spell or she had a speech impediment, for her responses were limited to "yes" and "no." When she tried to use the letters her best effort was the tedious repetition of E, F, F — a message meaningless to us.

One evening in August, Hettie put on a new act, one which I believe may be unique: She apparently invaded a candle! About 9:00 on the evening of August 21, 1968, after a fruitless struggle with the uncommunicative Hettie, I noticed that one of the candles was acting strangely. Its flame flickered wildly and flared as high as three or four inches.

"Martha Ann," I said, "look at that candle. I think we're having some kind of manifestation." As I spoke the flame leaned toward us and made what seemed to be a beckoning motion.

We immediately checked to be sure no draft was causing this.

Martha and I moved closer to the candle and I asked, "Hettie, are you in the candle?" The flame shot up to five inches and flickered from side to side. This gave me a clue. I asked Hettie to make the flame high for "yes" and low for "no."

Now we could converse with the otherwise speechless Hettie. We learned she had been raised on a farm and never had learned to spell. "E. F. F.," it turned out, were the initials of her minister, whom she adored.

Now we began a period of experimenting with Hettie. When we played a music box the candle flame danced gracefully to "Clair de Lune" and became lively in time with "The Blue Danube."

To our amazement, when we suggested Hettie take a bow she did; the flame bent toward us and leaned over. The statue of an angel stood behind the candlestick. When we asked Hettie if she could see it the flame leaned over backward. Next we asked her if she could inhabit two flames at once. The other candle immediately began to perform.

This entire performance was remarkable because it appeared that the candle was animated by a thinking being. The movements of the flame could not have been accidental.

We have continued to communicate with Hettie, of course, using different candles from day to day. We have continued to get the same results.

We've used up many candles — and Hettie is still with us. We believe she's a special spirit who is in her element when aflame.

> — *Esther Whitby, Philadelphia, Pennsylvania*
> *August 1969*

Pennies from Heaven

I had always been skeptical about Ouija board messages until last year. Then I had a change of heart. Often my daughter Kay and I used to sit down and ask questions of the Ouija board just for the fun of it.

On the evening of May 27, 1965, about 9:00 P.M., I made a pot of coffee and brought out some cookies and Kay and I sat down at our old solid oak table in the kitchen for some fun with the board.

The planchette moved around the board and then began to spell out, "Marianna, you will soon have money roll in from everywhere. We will start you with a blessed coin."

As the word "coin" was completed, a penny dropped to the board, from the bottom of the planchette. Now, before we started asking questions of the board, I had polished it with a soft cloth and also had wiped the feet of the planchette to get rid of any dust and to make it move more easily. If a penny had been stuck in some way to the bottom of the planchette, a most unlikely possibility, I surely would have seen it or dislodged it in preparing for our evening's fun.

Thus, when the penny dropped to the board, Kay and I looked at each other in startled amazement. We were even more baffled when the planchette went on to spell out, "Big oaks from little acorns grow," a phrase I often repeat to myself when I drop pennies into a jar in which I save them. The planchette continued to spell: "We love you. The coin will draw money to you like a magnet. Have faith in it."

I always have liked lilacs and since it was lilac time, I jokingly said, "If you can fetch a coin, why not a lilac for me?"

The planchette spelled, "What more do you want, you of little faith?" At that instant a nickel dropped onto the floor beneath the kitchen window on the far side of the room. Then, to our astonishment, a strong floral scent wafted up from the table. It kept getting stronger until I was compelled to ask what it was.

The Ouija then spelled out that the table had been magnetized and then, instead of the customary movement of the planchette, the whole board started twirling and twisting beneath our hands.

Kay jumped up and said, "Let's stop this and get out of this kitchen!"

We don't know to this day what was happening but we agreed to stay away from the Ouija board — at least until our curiosity once more gets the better of us.

— *Marianna Wade, Bellflower, California*
January 1967

"You'll Be Moving..."

I see you moving from that house you're in at present," the fortuneteller said, after spreading the cards and poring over them. "Impossible," I said. "We'd never move from our house in Mosman. We all love it — near the sea, shops, schools, transport. Surely you're mistaken."

"No, you'll be moving before this year is out," the woman said.

"But how? Why?" My voice was tentative, for Mrs. Marriott is a renowned clairvoyant in Sydney, and her predictions about famous people are widely published in Australian magazines. She was less well known when I saw her in 1977 but today people wait months for appointments with her.

"Shuffle the cards again, dear," she said. "We'll try to find out."

Nervously I started shuffling. One of the cards fell to the floor. It was a king, a dark card.

"Ah, what falls to the floor comes to the door," she said. "A dark man."

Romance? Tall, dark and handsome? A bit late making an appearance, I thought, but better late than never. I had been alone a long time.

"Can you tell me a little about him?" I ventured.

"You don't want to leave but you will," she said.

Well, perhaps his home would be larger than the one I shared with my children. I hoped he would live near the sea. I'd have only a small wedding reception this time and I'd wear blue ... no, maybe pink.

"Shall I remarry then?" I asked.

Briskly stacking the cards, Mrs. Marriott said rather peevishly, "I've told you all I can see."

I handed her the figure agreed upon and got up to leave. Then she added, almost like an afterthought, "The house you'll move to will be farther back from the road." I wanted to ask more but her attitude didn't encourage questions.

My children laughed when I told them.

"You're mad, Mum, going to a fortune teller!"

We soon forgot the incident until three months later when a man came to the door.

"Are you the owner of this property?"

"Why do you ask?" I was cautious. Probably he was just a real-estate agent, looking for homes to sell in our area.

"I'm from the Mosman Council and I'm afraid I have some rather disturbing news for you. Your house is one of those on our list for resumption in this area." This meant the city wanted my property for some municipal use. I was stunned and I just stared at the man.

"We will, of course, give you market value," he said reassuringly.

"But I don't want to move!"

"I think it would be advisable to accept our offer. If you remain once all the other homes have been resumed, you'd have Council trucks everywhere. We're making this a substation, you see. These are all very old homes around here that probably don't meet present-day building requirements. If you look at it in the right light, this is an excellent opportunity for you. Other owners we have approached have all agreed to sell."

"And if I wait?"

"Well, later we couldn't offer you today's prices because by then your house would have dropped in value. In fact, nobody would buy it. The Council is quite reasonable in these matters. You'll have time to find other accommodations and I think you'll find our offer quite fair."

"I'd like to think about it, nevertheless, and see my solicitor."

"Of course," he said agreeably, giving me his card.

Within six months of seeing the tall, dark man disappearing down my garden path and before the year was up we had moved. It didn't occur to me until we were settled into the other house that it was in fact much farther back from the road.

— *Erica Condon, Chatswood, N.S.W., Australia*
April 1981

THEY HAD A HUNCH

The first person had gone through and the second was handing his ticket to the conductor when suddenly I panicked. I felt a cold chill creep from the nape of my neck down my spine. My hand that held the ticket was shaking, and it seemed I couldn't move an inch. But I knew I must get out of that line!
— From Helen Harriet O'Mara's "How Did I Know?," page 83

Abraham Lincoln had several premonitions of his impending death, including a dream six weeks before his assassination of mourners surrounding his casket. Journalist William Stead thought he would die at the hands of a mob. Instead, he died in 1912 with a mob — aboard the *Titanic*. Stead also wrote the story "Majestic" in 1892 about a ship that sinks in the Atlantic after hitting an iceberg. We can't say for certain what power permits us to avoid future catastrophes or guess the outcome of unfolding events, but perhaps we would benefit from paying more attention to our hunches, as the following stories demonstrate.

How Did I Know?

I had left Long Island College Hospital School of Nursing where I was a student, and I was on my way home for a 30-day vacation. I took the subway to Grand Central station where I picked up my reservation on my way to northern New York State, where my family lives. My thoughts were entirely on the 30 days ahead and the delight of doing as I pleased for the next four weeks. After my long months of life as a student nurse, a reunion with my affectionate family would be a welcome relief.

I hadn't stood by the big clock in the center of Grand Central station more than five minutes when the gate slid back and the bored, tired, but still amiable ticket conductor called, "All aboard!"

In spite of my readiness, three people were ahead of me in line to board the NYC Lake Shore Limited. I took my place in line, my ticket clutched firmly in my left hand, my bulging suitcase in my right.

The first person had gone through and the second was handing his ticket to the conductor when suddenly I panicked.

I felt a cold chill creep from the nape of my neck down my spine. My hand that held the ticket was shaking, and it seemed I couldn't move an inch. But I knew I must get out of that line!

I turned, mumbling, "Excuse me, please," and bumbled back toward the safety of the big terminal floor. People stared at me as I almost ran to the Big Clock. I leaned my back against the marble shelf. No sooner had I done this, feeling a relief beyond words and not knowing why, than I began to tremble all over. The terminal had not seemed warm before but now perspiration trickled down my face. My hands were slippery wet. My suitcase slid to the floor and I just stood there! I didn't care how I looked or who looked at me. This was the place for me — not in the line leading to the Lake Shore Limited. I must not take that train!

My family expected me at 7:30 the following morning and now, since I had no intention of taking that train, I would have to call home. I decided that after the train pulled out I would tell them that the train was gone but that I would take the morning train. I checked my bag in an overnight locker, deciding that I had best return to the Nurses' Home for the night.

I called home and my mother answered. I told her the train had left but that I would get on the morning train without fail.

Mother said, "Oh, Helen, we're so disappointed. We were all figuring that in about 12 hours you would be here. Now we'll have to wait until night. What are you going to do now?"

"Well, I've checked my bag and I'm going back to the Nurses' Home. I'll stay there tonight. I'll tell you all about it tomorrow night," I said.

"What do you mean, Helen?" Mother asked.

"I don't know, yet. But watch tomorrow's paper."

I continued talking to Mother a few moments more, at the same time wondering what I meant by these strange remarks.

I went back to the Nurses' Home. I don't remember that my sleep was restless that night. In fact, I have a dim recollection of being thankful that I was in my hideous room, and that I found it wonderfully welcoming for once. I was indeed thankful, but I didn't know why.

I awoke at 6:00 A.M., hurriedly dressed, signed out again and ran to Joe Ralskil's corner drugstore where I bought a newspaper. The headlines screamed: "NYC Lake Shore Limited Leaves Track At Little Falls!"

There followed an account of the tragedy in which a high school friend of mine, Jimmie Tallon, was killed, along with many other passengers and crew members. The train had left the tracks shortly before midnight on April 19, 1940. It plunged across a highway and into a rock embankment. Pullman cars were ripped open, smashed and piled along the right of way.

Another strange experience for me! I wonder how I know about these approaching tragedies ahead of time. Through the years my premonitions have concerned events involving me meeting or missing persons whom I should meet or miss. I still "play my hunches" even though it often seems silly at the time. But how do I know?

— *Helen Harriet O'Mara, Syracuse, New York*
October 1960

A Bullet in the Baby's Crib

On August 20, 1953, I was to babysit the small daughter of Phyliss and Albert Ilko. After arriving at their home on 44th Street in Cleveland, Ohio, I sat down on the couch and proceeded to do my eighth-grade homework.

I had such a weird, uneasy feeling, though, that I had to put my homework aside. After praying to God to help me understand what he was trying to tell me, I inspected the entire house — the doors, the stove, and areas where there might have been a hidden fire.

Then, as if God Himself were pushing me, I felt impelled to go to the baby's room. The baby was sleeping peacefully, but on impulse I picked her up and held her close.

Seconds later I heard terribly loud noises, "Bang! Bang!" It seemed to me as if something had whizzed past my face, very close and very fast. For a few seconds I stood there immobile, clutching the child tightly. When I regained my senses I turned on the light and began checking the room.

When I looked in the crib I could not believe my eyes. Exactly where the baby had been sleeping so peacefully was a hole — a bullet hole.

Frantically I called my parents. My father came immediately and confirmed that it was a bullet hole. Then we called Mr. and Mrs. Ilko and the police.

Investigation disclosed another bullet had lodged in the wall. The man upstairs in this two-family home had decided, while intoxicated, to clean his guns. In his condition he was not aware that one was loaded, and it had discharged.

Had the child been in the crib, she would have been killed instantly. The parents and I both thanked God for having spared her. Was it extrasensory perception? I call it a miracle.

— *Gloria Ashworth, Brooklyn Heights, Ohio*
March 1965

An Earth-Shaking Premonition

Something awful is going to happen to San Francisco," my sister Kate said when she returned on Friday, April 13, 1906, to Nevada City, California, where she lived with my husband and me.

She told me she had said the same thing to the ticket agent when she left and he had said, "Miss, aren't you choosing an unlucky day to travel?" She replied, "No, I think I'm taking a lucky day to travel because something awful is going to happen to San Francisco." He had only laughed at her.

Then she said, "You know, Jo, I never was so glad to get out of San Francisco." I was more than astonished because she actually never had been glad to leave San Francisco at any time. She loved the great city and always stayed as long as she could. She loved shopping, too, and my husband Harry had given her $200 to buy a wardrobe for the baby I expected in July. Kate had come back with only a few of the things we needed for the baby. This behavior was most unlike her.

On this visit to San Francisco, Kate had stayed at a rooming house on California Street run by a Mrs. Lambert. On Thursday night, Kate reported to me, she got up and looked out the second-story window at the lights of the city. A chill came over her. She shuddered and said aloud, "Poor San Francisco!"

When she told Mrs. Lambert about it in the morning, she insisted it wasn't a dream. "I have a premonition," she said.

Mrs. Lambert had been thinking of going to New York to visit her daughters. She said to Kate, "If there's anything to your feeling I might as well go now." She packed and left that day.

Five days later the house had sunk two stories deep into the Earth.

But the Friday Kate returned home, Harry laughed at her as she repeated her story for him and added more detail.

"I couldn't wait for the dress I bought. It's being altered at the shop. It needed to be shortened a little. I also had to leave the wild-cat," she told him. "I just couldn't wait while it was stuffed." Harry was a little put out about not getting his stuffed wildcat but he took this in stride, continuing to laugh at Kate's fears.

Five days later, about six o'clock in the morning — the 18th of

April, 1906 — our house in Nevada City began to shake. Tables overturned and dishes fell from the shelves. Kate jumped out of bed and came running downstairs. The first thing she said was a repetition of her week-old phrase: "Poor San Francisco!"

Within two hours we had the news that an earthquake had left San Francisco in burning ruins.

> — *Josephine Allen Gray, La Crescenta, California*
> *May 1967*

Fated to Marry?

When I was a child of 10, I lived in a city in southern Indiana upon the shores of the Ohio river. I liked to play with paper dolls, and named all of my boy dolls Le Roy — although I knew no one by that name. But one day without any apparent reason I changed the name of all my boy dolls to Allen, and Allen they remained so long as I played with them.

I did not know that in another town in Indiana, at least 100 miles away, which neither I nor any member of my family had ever visited, there was living a young man who, 15 years later, was to become my husband. His name was Le Roy but when he was in his twenties he suddenly changed it and adopted his mother's maiden name of Allen — the name by which he was known from the time I met him until the time of his death.

How did a little girl, playing with her dolls in a walled garden, know these things and reflect them in her play? As nearly as I am able to reckon, I must have made this change with my paper "family" just about the same time that Allen, then a young man, made the change for himself. I can remember that it seemed important but I did not know why — at that time.

> — *Louise Wood, Indianapolis, Indiana*
> *March 1951*

My Father's Hunch

When I was a boy my family lived in Lodi, Wisconsin, a town with a population of about 500 at that time (1888) and a trading center for the surrounding farms. Everyone knew everyone else for miles around and they trusted one another.

Lodi, like most small towns in those days, had no bank and financial transactions were handled largely through postal channels. A few of the merchants had small safes in which they kept important papers, bonds, notes and cash. My father, Absolom Van Deusen, was in the furniture and undertaking business and he had such a safe. One day an elderly widow came to my father and asked if he would keep her money in his safe — a total of $300. She said her 30-year-old son was overly fond of liquor and seldom worked. He was living with her and she was afraid to leave any money around her home for fear he would find it and spend it for drink.

Father agreed to keep the money for her on the condition that he would not be held responsible for it in the event that something happened. I was only eight years old so I can't recall whether it was days, weeks, or months that passed before my father had a hunch he had better return the widow's money.

Late that afternoon he emptied his safe, returned the $300 to the widow, and took his own cash and papers home. In the grip of his strong intuition he left the safe unlocked, thinking if robbers paid him a call they then would do little or no damage.

The next morning as he walked toward his store he met some of his friends who said excitedly, "Van! You'd better hurry to your store. It looks as if it's been broken into!" Father in reply said, "Boys, let's stop in at Sherm's and get some cigars. My treat!"

The men thought he was joking and took him by the arm to rush him on. When they entered the store and found the safe door wide open, Father grabbed his derby hat from his head, threw it to the ceiling and cried out, "Thank God, I followed my hunch! I took everything out of that safe last night. Now let's go get those cigars!"

— *William A. Van Deusen, Hollywood, California*
August 1968

Inner Warning

Thirty-four years ago I experienced one of the strangest and still unexplained events in my life. It was 1959 and my family was just sitting down to supper. The day had been a stormy one, with much lightning and thunder. At the table sat my father, Waymon Carter, my aunt, Cordelia Vincent, my baby brother, David Carter, and myself.

Suddenly, without saying a word, my aunt reached over and jerked my baby brother from his high chair. Within seconds of her movement, a ball of white light the size of a basketball, with a brightly burning yellow center, flew through the glass kitchen window without making a sound.

This ball of light passed directly through the center of my brother's high chair, which only seconds before was occupied by his tiny body. It then made a sharp turn to the right, passing directly in front of me and to the right of my father. Silently, it dropped to the floor, skipping much like a flat stone across water, and bounced out of the kitchen and through the wooden front door.

The entire event took place in silence; only after the ball of light passed through the door did we hear a loud explosion, followed by the entire house shaking on its foundation. No damage could be found, not in the glass window, the wooden high chair, the linoleum floor, or the wooden front door.

My aunt was later asked what made her take the action that she did, just seconds before the mysterious ball of light (which I now believe was ball lightning) entered our kitchen that afternoon. She could only explain that suddenly, an intense inner voice firmly and clearly instructed her to move immediately and pick up the baby, for something terrible was about to happen.

I do not know where that inner voice came from, but I have no doubt that, because my aunt did not question its urgency, my brother is alive today.

— *Sherry A. Larson, Live Oak, Texas*
April 1994

Mercy by Mail

I was a stewardess during the Korean airlift. I spent more time in the air than on the ground. Thus I had a good excuse for not writing letters, something I detest. My youngest sister, Wanda Lee Ball, was even more lax; since she had married and moved to Oregon she wrote so seldom that I did not even know her current address.

One night in Honolulu, however, I awoke with a strange and urgent compulsion to send my sister $75. I tried to ignore this feeling, for I was quite tired and had only a few hours before I was to fly to Tokyo. But I couldn't sleep, and so I finally got up and wrote a check. Still, I could not rest until I walked the half mile to the post office and mailed it. Then I fell into a deep sleep.

To this date I do not know what address I put on the envelope or how she got it. However, I received a prompt reply. When Wanda received my check she had been desperate; her husband had left her with a small baby, no food in the house, and no money for rent, fuel, or any necessity. To pay her debts and buy food she had needed exactly $75. My check was an answer to her prayer.

What we still cannot figure out, though, is how I sent the check to an address to which she had just moved.

— *Glennagere Messenger, Seattle, Washington*
December 1963

Message in Chalk

One afternoon in November 1974 I was tending my grandchildren because my daughter Margaret Carter was ill with influenza. It was getting on toward two o'clock and time to pick up Daniel from Emerson School where he attended first grade.

I noticed young Jared playing with the slate and chalk I had bought that morning for his brother. I realize most toddlers will play with anything within reach but I wanted Daniel's gift to look like new when he got home from school. So I took the chalk away from Jared and planned to take the slate to the kitchen to wash off his scribbles.

But they were not scribbles. In chalk was a command: "Take me home, now." I grabbed the baby and hurried to Margaret's house two blocks away.

She didn't respond to my ringing the doorbell so I entered anyway. I smelled gas which was escaping from a faulty heater. I set Jared on the porch and dragged Margaret from the couch into the fresh air. She soon regained consciousness.

I thank God for Jared's automatic writing and for the urge to buy a slate and chalk that morning.

— *Elizabeth Cole, Williams, Arizona*
August 1976

A Scent of Danger

During the 1969—70 school year I moved to the north shore of Oahu, 40 miles from Honolulu, Hawaii. My 17-year-old daughter, Manu, stayed in the city with friends at the Islander apartment complex to complete her senior year of high school, and I missed her.

One of my housemates made a pair of hanging lamps from large empty juice cans with Indian fabric glued around them. He fitted them with light bulbs and odds and ends of old wiring. When he plugged them in, they were beautiful, but I worried about the danger those old cords might create.

One night, when everyone was asleep, I was awakened suddenly by a flash of light, a loud pop, and the smell of smoke. I rushed to Bill's room and shouted, "Wake up! Check your lamps! I smell burning wires!"

"I unplugged them before I went to sleep," he growled sleepily. But I went from room to room, frantically waking everyone. The termite-ridden old house would burn in no time! Afraid to turn on the lights, I took my flashlight to check and unplug every electric appliance in the house.

There was no sign of fire, but the smell of smoke still filled my nostrils. I thought it must be the wiring in the attic.

No one else smelled smoke, and they were annoyed with me for waking them up. To humor me, one of the men grabbed my flashlight and climbed into the attic. "Nothing," he shouted. When he let himself down, he said, "Why did you have to wake up everyone else with your nightmare?"

My housemates returned to their beds and I went into the dark kitchen and made peppermint tea. I needed to relax. I wasn't certain anymore if I still smelled smoke or if it was just the memory of the nightmare. As I relaxed in the predawn stillness, the phone rang. I answered warily.

"Ma, I'm sorry to wake you up ...."

"Manu. It's all right. I was up anyway. The strangest thing happened ...." But my daughter interrupted. "I can't talk long because a lot of other people are waiting to use the phone. I just wanted to let you know we're okay, because I knew you'd worry if you heard about it on the morning news," she said.

"Heard about what?" I demanded, stiffening.

"About the fire at the Islander."

"Fire?" My nostrils prickled.

"The building burned down," she explained. "But everybody got out safely and we're at the laundromat."

"So that's what it was." I told her about the phantom that woke me. My daughter was quiet. Then she said, "You must have picked up on my panic when I ran out of the building. That just goes to show that no matter how far apart we are, you can still sense what's on my mind."

And so it proved for years afterward. No matter how far away she moved, I often knew when she needed me long before she telephoned.

— *Malie Sellers, Mountain View, Hawaii*
September 1996

Why I Quit My Job

In 1946, I was hired as a timberman and assigned to work with the cutter and scraper at the Harwick, Pennsylvania, coal mine owned by Duquesne Light Company. A timberman's job consists of setting posts and crossbeams to secure the roofs over working areas. We worked in a section designated "4 West," but after about five months the company transferred me to another section called "15 North."

When I went over to 15 North, a sense of fear immediately overcame me. It seemed even the dark damp walls were warning me, urging me to stay clear of the area. I felt some danger awaited me if I didn't heed my hunch, but I couldn't explain it. I was new to mining but I had felt at ease and safe working in 4 West.

When I told my foreman about my fear of 15 North he laughed and said, "That's just your imagination. It's perfectly safe." I talked to other men on the job about my feeling and they, too, told me it had to be my imagination.

The day before I was to report to work at 15 North a voice within me kept repeating, "Don't do it!"

I argued with the foreman the next day and finally he said, "You have two days to make up your mind. I need a timberman in 15 North. If you don't get over this foolish idea by that time there won't be a job for you."

I needed that job but I couldn't take it. I tried to convince myself that my feelings were absurd but I couldn't get over the fear. Something was going to happen in 15 North and I didn't want to be there when it did.

I quit. Two days later I was sitting at home reading when the shrill mine whistle blew. It was the dread signal of a mine accident. I looked out the window and saw an ambulance speeding toward the mine.

"Somebody has been hurt or killed," I said aloud, "and I know exactly where."

A little while later I walked over to the mine and asked the first person I met what had happened.

"Three men were killed in section 15 North," he replied. "Roof caved in."

I later learned the dead men were the cutter, the scraper and the timberman.

— *Maurice R. Sonafelt, Lower Burrell, Pennsylvania*
November 1970

DREAM MESSAGES

She spent three months in a cast, and the leg gave her trouble for the rest of her life. She never again dismissed Grandfather's prophetic dreams.
— *From Renie Burghardt's "The Dream That Came True," page 97*

Most dreams are what mythologist Joseph Campbell called "little dreams." They are filled with the dreamer's own immediate priorities. The images are uppermost in the dreamer's mind: They are still fresh in his or her consciousness and their significance is immediate and forthcoming. There is no mystery here, no puzzle to pick apart.

Other dreams, "big dreams," baffle and astound us: Dreams of portent, dreams of clarification, dreams that offer a solution to a problem. Dreams may even anicipate the future. As Renie Burghardt and others have discovered, we would do well to pay attention to them.

The Dream That Came True

In the fall of 1947 my grandparents, Jozsef and Terez Szitak, and I escaped from Russian-occupied Hungary into neighboring Austria. Along with hundreds of other destitute Hungarians, we were taken to a displaced-persons camp.

Camp Spittal was dismal, with rows and rows of army barracks. However, just outside the camp was a beautiful world of mountains, clear, cold streams, and rolling, flower-carpeted hills. In the summer of 1948, when I was 11, my best friend Lenka and I discovered a huge crop of wild blueberries there. We gorged ourselves with the luscious berries and hurried back to camp to tell our families about them.

The following morning, Grandmother and I joined two other women and children and headed for the berry patch. We left bright and early, for it was a five-mile walk. Grandfather had tried to talk Grandmother out of going because he had dreamed that something terrible would happen. "Oh, you and your dreams," Grandmother said, and that was the end of that.

After almost three hours of walking, we finally reached the hill that had the berries on its lower side. As I ran excitedly down the hill ahead of everyone, I heard a loud crack. Then I heard Grandmother wail! Apparently, when she took a step to start down the hill, she slipped, and her right leg folded under her. The women tried to help her, but she wailed even louder. She couldn't be moved.

A few minutes later I was running up the dirt road for help. I knew Grandmother was in great pain, and I had a long way to go. As I ran, I prayed for a miracle, tears streaming down my face. "Oh, why hadn't we heeded Grandfather's warning?" I kept asking myself. Had he not kept us one step ahead of danger during World War II because of his prophetic dreams?

About halfway to camp, I finally stopped to rest for a minute, exhausted, when I heard a sound up ahead. Then I saw it. It was the army truck that was used as an ambulance at camp, and it was heading my way! The ambulance came to a stop at my side. Grandfather was sitting next to the driver.

As we drove back to get Grandmother, he explained that after we left, he had fallen asleep again. Suddenly, he had heard an awful cracking sound in his dream, and he had heard Grandmother cry out in pain. He went to the ambulance driver and told him that they had to go find Grandmother. "I begged him to go and see, and he finally agreed," Grandfather explained.

By the time we got Grandmother on the stretcher, her leg was blue and doubled in size. The bone that we heard crack was her tibia, and two small bones in her ankle were broken as well. She spent three months in a cast, and the leg gave her trouble for the rest of her life. She never again dismissed Grandfather's prophetic dreams.

— *Renie Burghardt, Doniphan, Missouri*
January 1997

Three Months from Today

Early one morning in 1966 I awoke from an unusual dream. I had been walking down a road that led down into a deep square cave, murky and damp, with a horrible musty smell. I saw water oozing down the gravelly walls in little streamlets and there seemed no way out.

I awoke with a start and sat on the edge of the bed pondering the dream. Suddenly a voice said, "Three months from today." Clearly and explicitly, the voice repeated, "Three months from today."

Puzzled, I went into the kitchen to look at the calendar. It was April 18. I counted three months to July 18 and circled the date.

"What is it? What's going to happen?" I kept asking myself.

My husband Henry came out to see what I was doing up so early.

"On July 18," I said, "something is going to happen." Then my flesh went clammy as if I still were trapped in my dream cave. My husband's steady blue eyes took in the circled date on the calendar, then he shrugged and suggested we have our coffee.

One morning a few days later, a neighbor, Mrs. Haines, came

in to visit. We were sitting in the living room when a spring blind came partly down over the window then jumped back as if someone had pulled it. The noise startled me but Mrs. Haines said, "Oh, that's nothing. Spring blinds often do that."

The spring months passed uneventfully except that on two occasions the blinds came down and snapped back as if drawn by a human hand. The last time it happened was about a week before the circled date on the calendar. My husband arose in the night to get a drink of water and the blind over the kitchen window came down and went back. Almost reluctantly, Henry told me about it the next week — on Sunday, July 17.

That night, after my husband had gone to bed, I knelt alone in prayer. As I prayed, a beautiful angel appeared before me with wings folded like the wings of a dove. What was God trying to convey to me?

It was already lunch when I remembered it was July 10. I mentioned it to Henry, saying, "Nothing happened." He didn't answer.

About three o'clock he made our usual tea, then said, "I'm going to lie down for a while."

"It will soon be time to put supper on so I'll stay here and read for a few minutes," I said.

About 20 minutes later as I went into the kitchen I heard a rattle in Henry's throat. I didn't pay any attention at first because he had bronchial trouble and I had grown accustomed to odd sounds in his breathing.

When I heard the second rattle, however, I knew it was different. I rushed to his bedside, lifted him and massaged his chest. Then I lay him back and ran to phone the doctor. When he arrived my husband was dead.

My son took me to his home and wanted the doctor to give me a sedative to relieve my shock. Despite all their coaxing I refused. That night as I sat on the edge of my bed, sleepless, I saw a vision of silvery white birds. The voice that had spoken three months before appeared again and said, "He arrived there safely."

— *Rebecca Hoffner, Vancouver, B.C., Canada*
- *February 1970*

On the Alert

I don't want to cause your father needless anxiety by telling him about a mere dream," my mother said, "but now that it has occurred three nights in succession, I feel so disturbed that I simply have to tell someone."

Some 50 years ago I was only a child, but I understood my mother Caroline's reticence about disturbing my father. James Petersen was a busy man, a stamp dealer with an office on Nassau Street in New York City.

"I dreamed," Mother continued, "that John Keller, your father's competitor, entered Dad's office accompanied by a stranger. He named certain rare stamps he said he was interested in buying. When your dad turned his back to get them from the safe, John dropped a stamp on the floor.

"The stranger saw this happen, picked up the stamp, examined it and claimed that it was counterfeit. Announcing that he was a detective, he arrested your father."

At that point in her dream, Mother always awoke. It was repeated in the same way, she said, on three successive nights.

That evening at dinner I noticed Dad looked at Mother several times in a searching manner. Then he asked, "What's troubling you? You haven't been yourself for three days."

"Oh, it's nothing but a silly dream," she replied.

"If you tell it, you'll feel better. Come on, out with it!"

As Mother recounted the dream Dad turned pale. For a moment he seemed unable to speak. Then he said softly, as if speaking to himself, "So that's what his game was."

Turning to Mother he demanded, "Why didn't you tell me right away? Part of your dream actually happened. John did come in with a stranger and he asked for those stamps. But as I started to go to the safe for them I thought it was an odd request. I knew John had not collected them before.

"I turned around to ask him when he had become interested in them and as I turned I saw him drop a stamp. Without suspecting any evil intention I said, 'You dropped something, John.' He said he had not, so I pointed to the floor. 'See, there is a stamp. I saw you drop it.'

"John seemed confused. He looked at his watch and said, 'It's later than I thought. I have an appointment. I'll have to see you at some later date.'

"I thought both men left rather hurriedly. I picked up the stamp he had dropped and wondered why he had not even waited to take it. Your dream answers the question.

"John has been tricky before but I didn't think he would try anything as bad as trying to get me in trouble. You should have told me. What if I hadn't turned around at the moment he dropped the stamp? Your dream would have warned me to be on the alert."

— *Carol A. Petersen, Richmond Hills, New York*
April 1970

A Childhood Dream

When I was a small girl every time I slept in a strange house I had the same terrible dream. I dreamed two men were driving down a road in an old Model T Ford with no top. The men got into a fight and the driver knocked the other man out of the car. The one who was knocked out of the car had a shotgun. He sat there in the middle of the road where he had fallen, raised the shotgun and shot the driver's head completely off. The man's head rolled grotesquely off his neck and over to the side of the road.

Each time I had this dream I was terrified and told it to my mother repeatedly. But she always said to forget it, it was just a nightmare.

The year I was 11, in 1937, my great-uncle, Gib Storey, was driving home after selling some turkeys. He had about $80 in his pocket which, at that time, was a lot of money. As he drove his Model T near Datto, Arkansas, he picked up a hitchhiker. The hitchhiker had a gun and tried to rob my uncle. In the scuffle the gun went off. My uncle's head actually was blown off.

The hitchhiker took the money and left my uncle's body in the car. He never was caught although in later years I understand it became common knowledge who he was.

After that, I never had the dream again.

— *Marjorie Yost (as told to Larrie Kay Yost),*
Victorville, California
August 1964

The Answer to a Prayer

I am not exactly young anymore and I often have viewed the changing times with awe. But one thing that never changes is prayer. On an isolated farm in the midwest, my siblings and I learned about prayer through a rare experience.

It was a cold winter day in 1922. My younger brother, Edward Brown, and I drove a horse and buggy to our little rural school two miles from our home in Dunn County, North Dakota. During the noon hour our teacher, Mrs. Nellie Barnett, asked us to drive to the neighborhood mailbox. It was three miles farther than our home. Even though I knew my father would be unhappy to have us do this, I wanted to please my teacher, so I did her bidding. And hoping to make Father realize I was responsible enough to handle his mail I also brought along the mail addressed to our house.

That was at noon. When school was dismissed at 3:30 P.M., the wind was coming from the north and snow filled the air. My brother and I hitched up Old Dan and started for home. We wrapped ourselves and our precious mail in a cowhide robe and headed into the storm. By the time we stepped from the buggy in the farmyard, snow encrusted our eyebrows and eyelashes, and our fingers and toes were thoroughly chilled. My brother went on into the house while I unhitched Dan and took him to the barn.

I returned to the buggy to pick up my lunch pail and the mail, and carry it into the house. But the robe had fallen to the floor; the mail was gone! The wind was blowing in vicious gusts and by this time even the robe was soggy with snow. My fingers felt like they were freezing, but the terror of losing four precious letters was freezing my very heart. I groped around the barnyard in the semi-dusk, looking everywhere. Finally it got dark and there was nothing left to do but go into the house and tell my parents what had happened.

My heart was pounding and my conscience was torturing me. Why had I disobeyed in the beginning? I knew it was forbidden to touch the mail. It also was forbidden to drive anywhere except to school and home. With panic in my heart I finally dragged myself into the house and admitted my guilt.

Perhaps my parents sensed my terror. At least I was not punished as severely as I had anticipated. This, however, did not ease my conscience.

Bedtime came — time for prayers. And then at long last I thought about God. There was the usual child's prayer and the Lord's Prayer. Then suddenly prayer became real and I added my own plea for help: "Please, God, help me find those letters. Please, please." I prayed myself to a fitful sleep. I would almost awaken and momentarily return to my pleading with God. Then at last real sleep came. And with it came a real dream.

In this dream I saw the old stone pile, behind the spot where the buggy typically sat. There, blown up against the stones, was a letter. Still dreaming, I saw another letter lying on top of the snow a short distance farther on. I searched on and, in the teeth of an almost snow-covered harrow, still a third letter had been caught. Then it seemed that I wandered a long time and finally came into a field where many Russian thistles had blown against a fence hedged by some Juneberry trees. There, among the thistles, lay the fourth lost letter.

Morning came and the dream was as fresh in my mind as the guilt was in my heart. Hurriedly I dressed in warm clothes and began my search before breakfast. A prayer remained on my lips as I ran toward the barnyard. Imagine my relief and thankfulness when I found every piece of mail exactly where it had appeared to me in my dream.

This happened 47 years ago but I am sure God still works His miracles for those who really pray.

— *Elizabeth Leroy, Fargo, North Dakota*
January 1970

VOICES OF WARNING

We never figured out how she heard my warning with all the distance between us. We do know that if it hadn't happened, she would have opened her door that night to an insane killer.
— *From Roberta Mae Brown's "Night Caller," page 111*

Instances of people hearing disembodied voices have been recorded throughout history, from the Biblical Saul in Acts 9:4-7 to St. Francis and Joan of Arc. In recent times, individuals and groups — such as International Network for Instrumental Transcommunication in Boulder, Colorado — even have tried to record spirit voices. Although the voices most often give reassurances, warnings, or similarly helpful messages, society as a whole still equates the hearing of voices with insanity. In the very first issue of FATE, G. H. Irwin noted that, according to one report, one in seven people in the U.S. heard voices in their head. Irwin said that the voices followed a pattern of "...threatening bodily harm, of ridicule, and of an almost diabolical insistence on performing acts of violence and destruction ... There seems to be a potentiality for trouble that may crop up in horrible form in one out of seven of our population. Even if this figure is grossly overestimated, the facts are frightening enough."

For those whose lives were saved by a timely warning, the disembodied voices are far from frightening.

A Cup of Tea

My mother, Mrs. Laurelle Gilmour of Blenheim, New Zealand, has had many psychic experiences but this one impresses me the most.

Our home is very old and from the front door you can look straight down the hallway through the lounge, to see whoever is working at the sink in the kitchen.

Mum was standing at the sink doing dishes and daydreaming when a voice, which came from within, told her to turn around very slowly and offer him a cup of tea! She couldn't believe what she had heard and just shook her head. But again this voice, insisting this time, told her to turn around very slowly, not to be frightened and to offer him a cup of tea!

A man had escaped from a mental institution about 80 miles from the house. Mum had no prior knowledge of this. Nevertheless, by this time she was very frightened and felt the hair on the back of her neck prickling. She turned around and couldn't believe it — there was a man standing right behind her. She hadn't even heard him come through the screen door.

Anyway, she offered him a cup of tea, not wanting to let on how terrified she was. She sat him down at the table, made the tea and poured out two cups, one for herself and one for this man. After seeing him start to drink his tea, she excused herself to check on her baby in the front bedroom. Once out of his sight she scooped up her baby and ran across the street to her good friend Aunt Molly. Mum told her to ring the police.

"Slip Robinson is in my kitchen!" she screamed.

Aunt Molly told her to stop being stupid, that he was in the mental institution. But Mum begged her to call, so she did.

The police arrived and blocked off all the exits in the immediate neighborhood, went inside our house, and brought him out.

The police inspector couldn't believe what he saw and asked Mum if she knew he was sitting down drinking tea as if he owned the place.

Mum said, "Yes, did I do wrong?"

The officer said, "No, Mrs. Gilmour, on the contrary, you couldn't have done anything better!"

When Mum asked why, he told her that this man had such an addiction for tea he was like an alcoholic, that after chopping wood for a woman in one of our suburbs he had asked her for a cup of tea and when she refused he went crazy and killed her with an axe.

We don't know who or what helped Mum but we thank God. And perhaps she inadvertently saved the life of another woman who wouldn't have been forewarned.

> — *Nicola J. Hoskin, Blenheim, New Zealand*
> *October 1978*

"Put the Carriage Back"

I was never one to believe in strange or psychic happenings. A pragmatist, I was always looking for logical, obvious answers. My first-born child, John Brown, was the apple of my eye. Staying home to care for him, I adored and cherished every moment, except for the late night and early morning feedings.

One nice day I tucked my little son into his baby carriage for a walk. Along the way I planned to do a few errands, pick up some items at the corner store, and stop by the bank.

The traffic was quite heavy and I had to wait at the corner of an intersection after leaving the bank, my final errand. It was warm and the sun was bright, causing me to squint. I gently lifted the carriage down from the sidewalk to begin crossing the street. I didn't see any vehicles coming.

Suddenly, a strong, firm, masculine voice commanded, "Put the carriage back on the sidewalk." Startled, I quickly obeyed, not questioning the voice for an instant.

Once back on the sidewalk, I backed up away from the curb. I don't know why. At that instant a tractor-trailer truck turned down that street, going too fast. He cut the corner so close that his rear tires came up over the sidewalk, missing my carriage only by inches!

I stood there stunned. For an instant, my mind visualized the carriage as it had been seconds before, being crushed by the truck. Then I reached for my baby. He was sound asleep, looking like an angel.

As I glanced around, I saw no one nearby. The voice I had heard came from somewhere else, like an echo inside my head. I hurried home. I have since learned that there was a tractor-trailer driving school nearby.

My son is grown now. I told him this story the last time he came home to visit. He's still the apple of my eye.

— *Mary Ellen Brown, Pittsfield, New Hampshire*
March 1994

Grandmother's Warning

Everyone in my family has seen ghosts. My brother, Paul, saw the ghost of a young girl dressed in Victorian clothes walking through his house. My mother, Frances, saw blue lights darting around her bedroom, and my dad, Terry, once saw the ghost of an elderly Chinese man when he was staying at his grandparents'. Those stories pale, however, in comparison to a ghost that appeared to both me and my father in April 1981 — and saved our lives.

I was 18 and living with my parents on a barge moored on London's Regents Canal. One night I was asleep in my small cabin, situated at the front of the barge. Around 2 A.M. I awoke with a start. I distinctly heard my Grandmother Irene.

"It's my birthday today," she said. It was indeed her birthday, but she had died the year before.

I looked around the darkened cabin. Everything was quiet and I could barely hear my parents at the other end of the barge, laughing at something on television. Because it all seemed so natural and because I had loved my grandmother, I wasn't frightened.

Instead, I was curious. I had no doubt that the voice I'd heard had belonged to my grandmother, but there was no one there. So where was she?

Feeling brave, I said, "Granny, if you are here, show yourself." As I said this, a white misty shape appeared on the wall opposite my bunk. It shimmered and pulsated, and then turned into an image of Irene. She was smiling and wearing a white silk dress with a corsage of wonderful orange lilies pinned to her right shoulder. She looked like an angel.

I had watched her image for about 10 seconds when I was overcome by an incredible fatigue. As my head hit the pillow, I thought that some unseen force had caused my sleepiness.

Two hours later I awoke with a start, remembering what had happened. I was horrified — in real life I'm a scaredy cat where ghosts are concerned.

I jumped out of bed and ran screaming to my parents. They asked me what was wrong. I stuttered that Grandmother Irene had appeared in my cabin, and I vowed never to sleep there again.

At first my parents pooh-poohed my experience and told me I must have been dreaming. This only made me more adamant. I knew what I'd seen! Sensing that I wouldn't be so easily calmed, my mother looked at my father and said, "Terry, you'd better tell Sharon what you just told me."

He admitted that two hours before, he'd been watching television when he heard Grandmother Irene's voice telling him to check the mooring ropes.

At first my father hadn't wanted to leave the cozy warmth of the cabin, but when he got outside he was glad he did. During the night the heavy rain had eased. As a result, the canal's water level had dropped considerably, leaving our ropes tangled around the mooring poles and our barge half-suspended in the air. If Grandmother Irene hadn't appeared with her warning, our barge would have snapped its mooring ropes, capsized, and left us trapped beneath the murky depths of the canal.

There is no doubt in my mind that Irene's ghost appeared that night to warn my father. She saved me and my family from a cold and watery death. That she appeared to me as well makes this guardian angel story all the more special to me.

— *Sharon Campbell, London, England*
May 1997

Night Caller

I sat down to watch the 11 o'clock news while my roommate finished ironing. Immediately I fell into a light sleep and dreamed that a short, stocky man with a salt-and-pepper crew cut was fumbling with the screen door. I woke myself yelling, "Don't open that door!"

I felt foolish. My roommate was staring at me wildly. There was no one trying to open the door of our Louisville, Kentucky, apartment.

Then I realized that the door I had seen in my dream was the door of my sister's house in Nashville, Tennessee. I immediately telephoned to see if she was all right.

"The strangest thing just happened," she began.

She explained that she was alone in the house; her husband was working and her son Mike had gone to visit friends but was supposed to be home by 10 o'clock. (With the one-hour time difference, that was 11 o'clock Louisville time.) At 10 she heard someone at her door. Thinking it was Mike, she started to open the door for him.

"Then," she said, "I heard your voice call out clearly, 'Don't open that door!'"

She had stopped and called, "Mike?"

The night caller, evidently thinking she was calling for someone inside the house, turned and ran down the street. In the light she could see that he was a short, heavyset man with a crew cut.

A few minutes later Mike's friends brought him home. They had heard on the radio that a murderer had escaped from the hospital for the criminally insane and was believed to be in that area.

They sat down to watch television. A bulletin flashed on the screen, showing the man my sister had seen running from her porch. He had been captured on her street, near her house.

We never figured out how she heard my warning with all the distance between us. We do know that if it hadn't happened, she would have opened her door that night to an insane killer.

— *Roberta Mae Brown, Middletown, Kentucky*
February 1987

"Stop!"

I was picking wild raspberries one July afternoon in a forested area near my home. Near the bank of a river, several trees had fallen some years before, and the open, sunlit area was filled with the twining canes of raspberry bushes.

In less than an hour I had nearly filled the gallon bucket I carried. I turned toward the river's edge, where a path would quickly take me out of the forest.

Suddenly a voice cried "Stop!" I froze in my tracks. The warning had come from just behind and to my right, as if someone had shouted almost into my ear. I looked over my shoulder to see who had spoken. No one was there.

I'm hearing things, I thought. But I looked around me, seeking the source of the unknown voice and, more important, the hazard it sought to warn me against.

Directly in front of me, half-hidden by tall grass but right where my next footstep would have fallen had I not stopped, was a basketball-sized paper nest. Its surface was crawling with bald-faced hornets, among the most aggressive stinging insects in North America.

I backed away. As I headed for home I thought of the strange warning that had saved me.

Several years later, while studying a turn-of-the-century map, I discovered that the area near the raspberry patch once had been an Indian burial ground with more than 250 gravesites. Several early settlers, too, were laid to rest nearby, their graves commemorated by wooden markers that have long since rotted away.

Coincidence, perhaps. But I wonder: Whose voice came out of nowhere to warn me on that hot July afternoon?

— *David R. Moffatt, Eveleth, Minnesota*
May 1997

The Voice of the Forest

Bob Salton was a forester working in the office of Timber Management of Region III headquartered in Albuquerque, New Mexico. His work required many trips into the woods to inspect logging jobs and to appraise proposed logging areas.

He always used to say, "Don't worry about yourself when you're in the woods. We 'timber beasts' have a guardian angel who speaks up in time of danger." His experience bore this out.

One summer he went into the forest some miles south of Flagstaff, Arizona. He found a small clearing that seemed an ideal place to camp for the few days he would be there. When he returned to his camp on the third afternoon of his stay, he heard a rumble like a clap of thunder, and then a stentorian voice.

"Robert, you fool!" the voice said. "For an experienced forester you have picked a dangerous place to pitch your tent. Move it!"

Startled, Bob looked around. The skies were clear and he knew he was alone, but what he did see was that he carelessly had pitched his small tent beneath the tallest pine around. As he prepared his supper he mulled over the eerie command, then shrugged it off as a product of an overactive imagination. But he was uneasy. He just could not ignore that voice. Tired as he was, he moved his camp a couple of hundred yards across the clearing into a clump of oak trees.

At last everything was moved. Bob crawled rather sheepishly into his bedroll and fell into fitful sleep. A few hours later a tremendous crash and roar of wind-driven rain jolted him awake. He looked out. The pine tree across the clearing had been splintered and felled by a bolt of lightning. Had Bob ignored the command of the voice in the forest, he would not have survived to tell this story.

— *William L. Chapel, Tombstone, Arizona*
February 1970

Asleep at the Wheel

I n 1981, my son worked as a semi driver for a soft-drink company. He had to get to work by 4:30 A.M., load his truck, check out, and be on his way.

One morning, not long after he had started to drive, I was asleep in my bed — but I found myself sitting beside him in his truck. I looked over at him and he was falling asleep! I jabbed him as hard as I could with my elbow and shouted, "John! John! Wake up!" He did, but it wasn't long before he was nodding off again.

I repeatedly jabbed him with my elbow and yelled at him. I stayed with him until we came to a town, and then I found myself back home in bed.

At the time, he and his wife were living with me. When he came home at 10:30 that night, I said, "How come you couldn't stay awake today?" He looked at me, surprised, and asked, "How did you know?" I told him of my experience.

He said he had a bad headache when he left for work, so his wife gave him one of her migraine pills, which made him sleepy. He also said he remembered feeling like he was being poked in the side and hearing some kind of noise. He stopped on the outskirts of town, pulled his truck over, and went to sleep until noon. Then he finished his deliveries and came home.

I have been psychic all my life and experienced out-of-body travel since I was a child, but I never thought they were any more than dreams until I was older. Even so, I was surprised to find myself in my son's cab when I knew I was asleep in my bed.

— *Henrietta Rader, Las Vegas, Nevada*
June 1997

"Look Out!"

While I was a senior at Amherst Central High School in Snyder, New York, in 1951, my parents decided to take me to Florida for my Easter vacation. My dad, Forest Wolverton, loved to drive and we spent more hours on the road than my mother and I could stand.

Tired and hungry, we stopped at the first motel we came to. Needless to say it was not on a par with the Ritz. The beds were lumpy and the radiators clanked all night.

Because no one could sleep, we were on the road again by 6:00 A.M. Dad was traveling about 30 miles per hour down a winding road in West Virginia when a voice said, "Look out!"

My mother snapped, "For heaven's sake, Forest, I'm in no mood for your jokes!" As Dad swore that he wasn't teasing us, another voice screamed, "Look out!"

Dad leaned over to see if the radio was on. It wasn't. Mother opened the glove compartment because I said that's where I thought the voices were coming from. Before she could snap it shut, both voices wailed, "Look out!"

By this time we were too shaken to continue driving. Dad pulled the car over onto the soft shoulder. We had barely come to a full stop when a car going over 90 miles per hour came around the bend on the wrong side of the road.

If Dad hadn't acted when he did, we all would have been killed in a head-on collision. The voices will always be a mystery to our family — but we'll always be thankful for them.

— *Sally L. Harper, Snyder, New York*
December 1988

VISIONS OF DEATH

There was Joe sitting propped against a concourse pole, bleeding from the head, just as I had seen him three nights before.
— From A. Stephenson's "Death Strikes Twice," page 119

There is such a severity and finality to death that its strike seems to leave an image in the minds of the psychically sensitive. The impression is stronger than a hunch or a metaphorical vision; these people seem to have box seat at the theater of death. They may picture the circumstances surrounding a death before it occurs, or have a vision of someone long dead whose identity they only discover later. Others can identify graves of the deceased, although there are no markers. As the following stories show, the visions are rarely welcome, usually unexpected, and always unnerving.

Death Strikes Twice

A few years ago while I was handling mail and baggage at a Pittsburgh, Pennsylvania, railroad station, I saw a man killed three nights before it happened. A little after 9:00 P.M. the Number 9 passenger and mail train from Washington, D.C., was unloading. The train was scheduled for a 20-minute stopover.

During this time the engine was supposed to be uncoupled and switched out into the yards to pick up a baggage car load of mail, then switched back and recoupled for its trip to Chicago. A railroad worker known as Joe the Car Knocker had the job of coupling and uncoupling the engine.

On this particular night I had unloaded my four-wheeled electric buggy into the combination mail and baggage car. Returning along the concourse to the station, I noticed a railroad worker sitting slumped on the concourse with his back against an iron shed pole. His cap lay beside him and his head was drooped.

I stopped the buggy, got off, walked over and looked at him. It was Joe. Streams of blood were running down his face onto his work clothes. I spoke to him, but he seemed unconscious. While I stood looking at him, scores of passengers walked by to board the train.

What seemed odd to me was that no one seemed to notice Joe sitting there bleeding. Even Les Campbell, the Station Master, had walked by without a glance. He nodded to me but did not seem to notice Joe.

I got back on my buggy and started toward the station. On the way up I met our foreman Davy McCrea, and told him about Joe. "He needs a stretcher and a trip to the hospital," I said. "He's unconscious and bleeding from the head."

The boss excitedly asked where Joe was. About five poles down, I told him. As he started down I yelled that the station master was down there somewhere and should be notified. I parked my buggy near the baggage room and started back on foot. Halfway down the concourse I met the boss and the station master. The station master added he had just seen Joe crossing the tracks to his shanty right after he had coupled the engine.

We looked at each other. I said, "I even spoke to the guy. Come on down and I'll show you the pole where he is." When we got to the pole both the boss and the station master gave me a funny grin and walked away. I stood there stupefied. There was no sign of Joe, blood, or anything else, and the train was slowly moving out of the shed. I thought I must be going nuts.

However, when Number 9 pulled into the station three nights later I was delayed getting to the front end with my load of mail and baggage. As I headed down the concourse I noticed some excitement ahead. A railroad car inspector, quite pale and shaken, came running toward the station. "What's wrong?" I yelled.

He didn't stop but yelled back, "Joe the Car Knocker had his head crushed between the coupling links of the baggage car and the train."

I hurried down. There was Joe sitting propped against a concourse pole, bleeding from the head, just as I had seen him three nights before. He was dead before the ambulance arrived.

— *A. Stephenson, Coraopolis, Pennsylvania*
October 1963

Television Vision

I was raised in an atheist family in the small farm community of Springfield, Colorado. I was taught to look at the world with a scientific eye. My parents informed me that gods, ghosts, UFOs, and psychic phenomena were all bunk. I believed them — until I was 12 years old and saw something that changed my life.

It happened in the early fall of 1967. I was sitting alone in front of our black-and-white television watching my favorite show, "Combat," as Vic Morrow and his men shot at Germans from inside the ruins of an old brick farmhouse. The show cut off into a commercial. When "Combat" resumed, I noticed something different. There were three black men fighting with the army and somehow they got into a jungle. The German soldiers had all turned into Asians, Vic Morrow was gone and some redheaded kid was now giving the orders.

I was annoyed. Evidently, someone at the station had put the wrong film into the machine. Instead of running the rest of "Combat," the station had put on a movie about fighting the Japanese. I got up and walked over to the set, intending to turn it off. Then the platoon leader caught my eye. His hair was red! And the jungle was green! The battle was in color — but we had a black-and-white television!

As I stood frozen in amazement, I heard the redheaded soldier, who appeared to be in his late teens, tell his men to run for it as soon as he started firing. Then I watched the young leader crawl on his belly through the mud until he reached a small hill. The teenager stood up in the open and started firing his rifle. Nearly all the enemy soldiers must have whipped their rifles around and shot at the kid. Their bullets ripped him to pieces.

Suddenly my astonishment turned into horror. That redheaded teenager who was getting blown apart was my brother Frank! I ran into the kitchen to get my mother, but when I showed her the television, it had gone back to black-and-white and Vic Morrow was again fighting the Germans.

When my father came in from the field, I told him what I had seen. Both he and my mother assured me that I must have fallen asleep, that Frank was all right and that nothing would happen to him. I had just had a bad dream.

I forgot about the incident until weeks later, when two soldiers knocked on our door. My mother answered it. When I heard her crying, I went into the living room to see what was wrong. There I learned that Frank had been killed. The soldiers said he had sacrificed his own life to save his platoon. My brother was a hero, and the government gave my family a tiny medal.

Two months after the funeral, I reminded my parents of what I had seen on the television screen. They got angry at me and told me never to bring up the incident again. I never spoke a word about it to either of them after that.

Since that day my life has changed greatly. Instead of being an atheist, I have become a student of religion and the occult. And I no longer watch television alone.

— Wyatt Clay Kaldenberg, Idaho Falls, Idaho
August 1987

Face in the Flames

It was a gloomy day in October 1910. I had been left in charge of my small sister while my parents drove to the orchards some 10 miles from our little home in Earlington, Washington.

I watched my dad drive our big spring-bed wagon out of sight, feeling lonely and left out. Apple harvesting by people in our community was an annual affair in which I had always participated. But Mother had hesitated to take little carrot-topped Susan because the weather was bad. This meant that I would have to babysit and miss all the fun — not to mention the fried chicken and all the other goodies that would be spread on long tables under the apple trees.

Mother left a long list of chores for me to do, and her parting words were to "take good care of Susan, and have a good fire in the kitchen stove so I can start dinner right away." Then with a loving pat she climbed up beside Dad and my two younger brothers and soon they were out of sight.

Time went fast until the chores were completed. After that, with nothing to do but sit and watch the road for sight of the familiar wagon, it seemed the day would never end. The house seemed empty and gloomy and dark shadows lurked in every corner. It started to rain and at 4:30 P.M. it was beginning to get dark. I gathered Susan into my arms and went inside and sat by the kitchen stove, cuddling her close and rocking, back and forth, wishing the big wagon would come driving in. Even the light from the kerosene lamp didn't dispel the gloom that pervaded the room. I couldn't rid my young mind of the idea that something terrible was going to happen.

It was 5:00 before I heard the familiar grinding sound of wagon wheels in our driveway. Then, remembering Mother's orders about the hot fire, I set Susan down while I put wood in the grate of the big wood stove. I removed the lids and laid sticks of dry wood on the hot coals. Flames leaped up and just as I placed the last stick in the grate an agonizing, lingering scream rose into the air. The flames shot high above the top of the stove and clearly outlined in them was a man's face, a face I recognized, contorted in agony. This apparition lingered in the flames until the agonizing scream had died away. Then the flames subsided, dropping to the level of the grate. But I couldn't move a muscle or speak a word as I looked up at my ashen-faced father who, hearing the scream, had come racing in to see what had gone wrong.

It was Mother who restored sanity. "Put the stove lids on before you burn the house down!" she ordered. Her face was white also, for she, too, had seen and recognized the face in the flames. Dad mopped cold sweat from his face and began to replace the stove lids. "Something has happened to Ned," he said finally. "Something terrible!"

Communication was slow in those days and it was almost two weeks later that we received word from Little Rock, Arkansas, that Uncle Ned Clinkingbeard had perished in a fire that destroyed his log cabin at 5:00 P.M., October 12, 1910 — the exact time at which we had seen his face in the flames of our kitchen range and heard his agonizing screams thousands of miles away.

— *Kay Norton, Fontana, California*
September 1964

Death at a Distance

In the late summer of 1954, while vacationing in Canada, my husband and I stopped at Lake Louise. One morning while I was standing on the front steps of the Chateau admiring the beautiful turquoise color of the lake and the glacier-covered mountains in the distance, I suddenly saw three people, one right after the other, fall to their deaths in a crevasse.

Quickly I ran to the side of the building where the guide had his office and asked him if anyone was on the mountain.

"Yes, seven Mexican tourists," he replied. "They wanted me to take them but I refused because it is too dangerous. I still said 'no' when they insisted and they went without me."

"I just saw three people fall into the crevasse," I gasped, pointing as I spoke.

He said, "You couldn't have seen anyone fall at that distance. It is 20 miles away!"

"Nevertheless, I saw them," I replied. "Surely you still have time to save the others, if you hurry."

He left immediately.

That evening four Mexicans came into the dining room followed by the guide. The guide came directly to our table.

He said, "Those are the four men I rescued this afternoon."

"Yes," I said. "And I was right about the others?"

"You were right," he said, "but I do not understand how you knew."

He told us the party of seven had intended to stay a week, but in view of what had happened, the remaining four were leaving in the morning. He also said the Mexicans wanted the incident kept quiet.

My husband and I watched them leave the dining room some time later. They never at any time looked in my direction or attempted to speak to me. I doubt if they ever knew who saved their lives.

—*Catherine Beatty, Drexel Hill, Pennsylvania*
January 1970

Baby Picture

For many years, sketching and drawing have been my favorite pastimes. Not knowing when the urge to draw will strike, my sketchbook goes everywhere with me. In 1988, I created a picture that turned out to have quite a story attached to it.

It started one summer day when I dropped in on a friend for a quick visit. Since I hadn't seen Jan for a while, there was much news to catch up on. While we were chatting, I opened my sketchbook to work on a drawing I had begun. The picture was a modified version of a baby's photograph taken from a magazine advertisement. In my drawing, the baby's features were quite different from the original. At one point during our conversation, Jan got up to get something. When she returned and looked over my shoulder, she freaked. "Oh my God," Jan exclaimed. "Where did you get that picture you're drawing?"

I couldn't understand her reaction, but I explained the source to her. "I can't believe it. The picture looks just like Dingus' brother who died years ago," she said. Then she told me about her husband's little brother who had died. I was dumfounded, yet skeptical. No way, I thought, perhaps it's just Jan's imagination. I promised to give Jan the completed picture.

While I was at home working on the picture, I thought that maybe when I was finished, it would no longer look like the baby who had died. But when I returned and presented the drawing to Jan, her eyes misted and a big smile spread across her face. She said the picture was even better. It was an exact likeness, even to the color of the hair, of this little guy I had never met.

Soon the time arrived when Jan was to give her husband the drawing. The picture was matted and framed, and Jan was excited. I wasn't there when the moment arrived, so I was highly curious about the outcome. I didn't see Jan until a week later, so by the time I was able to ask her about the picture, I was beside myself. At first Jan would not say anything, but then she smiled. Dingus had burst into tears and wept when he saw the drawing, because, for all those years after the baby's death, Dingus had craved an image of his baby brother, but no photograph of the baby existed. It was the best gift anyone could have given him.

I saw Dingus a while ago and he kept reminding me about the picture. His mother had seen it and loved it. Dingus said that the picture travels with him on all his moves. It is one of his most prized possessions.

At first I was stunned, wondering how this had happened. Years later I realized that a special need had been met, and I am thankful and excited to have been part of meeting that need. It was wonderful to see how much happiness the picture gave Dingus and his mother. There is much more to the universe than meets the eye. The psychic flow can move in mysterious and odd ways to bring about good for others. Used in the right way, with the proper attitude, it is a valued gift.

— *Gloria Montgomery, Silverthorne, Colorado*
August 1996

A Private Showing

Just last year I was living in Philadelphia. On January 5, 1966, walking home from work about 10:00 P.M. I noticed figures moving around in a darkened candy store located a block from where I lived. I knew the store and its owner, an old man, and somehow I sensed something wasn't quite right. I went to the window and peered in.

I could make out the figure of the old man and I saw he was getting a terrible beating. A youth I recognized as one of the town hoods was hitting him on the head over and over again. Another boy stood at the cash register stuffing its contents into his pockets.

I yelled at them to stop and pounded with my fists on the plate glass window. Neither boy paid the least attention to me. One calmly continued to fill his pockets and the other held the old man up with one hand and savagely beat him with some sort of club. Horrified, I watched as the old man slumped to the floor, blood pouring from his head.

I ran to the door, frantically trying to get in. I found it locked and when I kicked and pounded the boys still ignored me. A puddle of blood formed under the old man and a thin stream crept along the floor and out beneath the door.

I ran the block home as fast as I could and called the police. My story came out in an excited babble but clearly enough that they got my name and address and the store's address.

A few minutes later two policemen came to my house and what they had to say really floored me. They told me nothing was amiss at the candy store. It had not been robbed, they found no evidence of any violence, and when they went to investigate they had awakened the old owner who had been peacefully asleep in his apartment at the rear of the store.

I could tell by the way they talked that they thought I was either a prankster or a drunk. They left, telling me I had better not pester a busy police department again or I'd be in trouble.

All the next day the scene I had witnessed and its bizarre outcome preyed on my mind. That night I walked two blocks out of my way to avoid passing the store. But when I reached home the same two policemen were waiting on my porch. They explained the candy store's owner had been robbed and murdered an hour earlier, his head beaten in just as I had described the night before.

Now they wanted the name of the boy I had thought I recognized. When he was brought in for questioning he confessed and implicated his friend. As I write this, they are in jail awaiting trial.

— *Mark Trevor, Chester, Pennsylvania*
April 1967

The Mask of Death

When I was a child of 12 a strange thing happened in my family. After supper one evening in October 1935, all of us except Father were seated around the fireplace in the parlor. He was sitting in the kitchen just finishing a late supper.

The lamps were not yet lit, although it was dark. We sat in the firelight in our home in Bradford, England. My mother was singing to my baby brother who was half asleep on her knee. My other brother and I played on the rug.

Mother's singing stopped abruptly. I looked up to see her gazing intently into the fire. Her face bore an expression of utter amazement. Instinctively my brother and I looked too. There, outlined by flames, deep in the red heart of the fire, was the face of a man, which was obscured by some kind of a mask he was wearing.

"Bill," my mother called over her shoulder. "Bill, come and look at this face in the fire." There came a disbelieving laugh from the kitchen but no father.

I jumped up, "Mom, Dad's just got to see this. I'll bring him." But no amount of pleading would induce Father to come into the parlor. He just laughed. When I got back to the parlor the face was gone.

Three weeks later my father was admitted to a hospital, dangerously ill from blood poisoning. In spite of all the extreme efforts to save his life, he died. While he was in the hospital the skin on his face erupted and, under doctor's orders, a mask was made from white gauze, saturated with medication and placed on his face. He died with that mask still on his face.

> — A. M. Antkiewicz, Clifton, New Jersey
> February 1963

Tragedy Lingers

This Packard's a steal at $300," the salesman beamed. "Three years old, one owner — a doctor — low mileage, and fine condition. A beauty, huh?"

My friend Lee Eckert and I, noting the classy black lines, deluxe beige upholstery, and toothy metal trimmings that were extra popular, agreed.

Earning $16 a week in 1935 at our first jobs, we craved a car.

"Take your time," he went on. "My telephone's ringing. I'll be back in a minute."

As Lee examined the outside, I leaned in to size up the car's interior and almost staggered. For a few seconds I felt submerged in a whirlpool of suffocating, gagging dark. I was thrashing while a force like quicksand dragged me into deeper, more overwhelming black — a point of no return, I knew.

Shaking, I scrambled out and grabbed Lee's arm.

"Something terrible happened in that car. I'm sure of it. Let's go."

A week later, Lucy Tart, a friend of my mother's, asked us to recommend a doctor. She told us that her family physician, a highly respected Dr. M., had been killed with his wife and two children about a month ago. His 1932 Packard had collided with a truck. All were so disfigured (the doctor had lost both eyes) that they required closed coffins.

His automobile was the dealer's sedan.

> — Wyn Esselborn, Newark, New Jersey
> January 1991

What Grandma Saw in the Graveyard

My Granny was one of those sweet, little old ladies that everyone loves. She was almost as round as she was tall, and she had snow-white hair, which she twisted tightly into a bun on top of her head. Although she brushed it neat, there were always several tiny curls that escaped the pins and fell at the nape of her neck. She told me these were her "Widow's Curls," and she had never had them until my grandfather died. I believed her, of course.

There was something strange about her eyes. I remember noticing it for the first time when I was about seven years old. They were a very pale blue. Sometimes they seemed to have almost no color at all. Sometimes I could see odd designs, etched in black, in the iris of her eyes. At other times a transparent film would cross them. When this happened, Granny didn't seem to hear or see anything around her.

I asked my father about it one day. All he said was, "Yes, Mother has strange ways sometimes." He told me that I mustn't bother her when she was in one of these moods. So, while I wondered about it, I was careful to do as he said. And I never questioned Granny about it.

By the time I was 10 I noticed that when Granny came to visit us, the neighbors wouldn't come near our house. I thought this was odd, because they were usually in and out of our house every day. They wouldn't permit their children to come to my house to play, either, until Granny left. They never objected to my playing at their houses though. I was as welcome as ever.

One day when Granny was visiting us and I was playing dolls at the home of one of my little girl friends, one of the children said, "I wish your grandmother would go home so we could come over to your house again."

I asked them why they didn't like my Granny.

"Why, don't you know?" Eloise said, her eyes very wide. "She's a witch!"

"She is not!" I yelled. "You're hateful. And you tell lies."

I ran home crying. I went into my room and threw myself on my bed. I didn't hear Granny enter the room, but I felt her hand on my shoulder. She asked me what was wrong. I sat up on the bed and threw myself into her arms. I asked her if it was true that she was a witch. She assured me she wasn't. Then, I asked her, why wouldn't she go into a graveyard?

"You are too young to understand these things," she said. "But the part about me seeing things that others can't see is true. A cemetery is a horrible place to me. Just don't you worry or feel bad about what the children said. Sometimes, when people don't understand the supernatural, they call those who do witches. When you are a little older I will explain a lot of things to you. You trust your old Granny, will you?"

I remember wondering what the supernatural was. I asked Mother about it. She said Granny claimed she could see the bodies of people buried in cemeteries hovering above the grass, in all stages of decay. From the way my Mother said it, I think she didn't believe it either. We didn't mention the subject again.

But when I was 14 something happened to make me wonder if it was true after all.

My grandmother lived in a small town in Tennessee. This story was told to us by my uncle, who was sheriff there.

A young man came to a nearby town about 30 miles from Granny's home, looking for his mother, whom he hadn't seen in 15 years. His mother and father had been divorced when he was quite young. She had married again and with her second husband had gone to live in this little town. The son had remained with his father, and he had heard very little from his mother in all these years. When he arrived, he found that his mother had died several months before. After her death, her second husband had left town. No one knew where to locate him. The young man wished to have her body exhumed and returned to her home town. He wanted to bury her in the family burial plot.

After the son received permission to remove his mother's body he found, to his dismay, that no marker had been placed on her grave. There were several unmarked graves in the little church cemetery and no one knew for sure which was hers.

Finally someone who knew Grandmother's reputation suggested asking for her help. At first she refused. But the son pleaded with her and she finally gave in. She went to the cemetery with him and my uncle, the county sheriff.

When they entered the graveyard, my uncle said, Granny turned as white as a sheet. She asked to see a photograph of the dead woman. After studying it for a moment, she pointed to a grave. It looked the same as the others, but she said, "That is your mother's grave." Then she turned and left as quickly as possible.

Both the son and my uncle were skeptical about opening the unmarked grave. But there was no other way to find out, so they chanced it. When the coffin was opened they found the body of the young man's mother.

Shortly after that my grandmother became ill. She lived all alone so we brought her to our home to look after her. I was asleep in my room one night when I was awakened by Granny. She told me she had come to kiss me good-bye. She said she was well now and was going home. She leaned over, kissed me, and told me to be good, that she would see me real soon. Before I had a chance to say anything, she turned and walked from the room.

I jumped out of bed and ran to the living room. I wanted to know why she was going home at that time of night and, also, how she had gotten well so fast. As I entered the living room I stopped short. My father was sitting in the big chair by the window. His head was in his hands, and I never will forget the terrible, hoarse sounds that came from his throat.

I ran into the guest room where Granny always slept. My mother was standing by the bed, crying too. Granny lay on the bed. I knew she was dead.

I went back to my room and found it was heavy with the scent of lavender — the only scent my grandmother ever used. And she had not been in my room in over four months — or did she really come to kiss me good-bye? Somehow, I think she did.

— *Robin Barrett, Long Beach, California*
October 1955

I Knew She Would Die

One day I was riding with my mother on a streetcar in Kansas City, Missouri. The car had elongated seats running its length with the passengers facing one another. I was not quite 10 years old.

My mother noticed me staring at a rather stout lady on the opposite seat and chided me, saying it was impolite to stare at a person. I whispered to her: "I can't help it. She's going to die when she gets off this car!"

We rode about 10 blocks. Then the stout lady stood up to get off at the next corner. As she got off, I jumped up, went across to kneel on the opposite seat and look out the window. My mother called me back. I turned and said, "I want to see how she dies!" I remember that quite a few people looked strangely at me.

I saw the stout lady alight from the car, walk over to the sidewalk and start to cross the intersecting street. She walked right into the path of a team of horses drawing a heavy wagon loaded with manhole covers. Since our car was not involved in the accident it moved on and I could see no more.

The *Kansas City Star* that evening reported the details and stated that the woman was killed instantly.

Later, my mother questioned me about my premonition. I simply said, "I knew she was going to die as soon as she got off the car; that's why I was looking at her!"

— *Reverend Florence Conners, St. Petersburg, Florida*
March 1951

The Storm

Late one afternoon in October 1920, I was driving on a dirt road leading into a small town in Wisconsin when a violent thunderstorm struck. I managed to get to a small restaurant, have supper, and get directions from the restaurant owner to the home of an acquaintance where I thought I could spend the night. There were no hotels. The rain was still coming down in sheets when I made it to my friend's front door and introduced myself to his wife.

She welcomed me with what seemed genuine relief and said that she was pleased to have a man in the house on a wild night like this. Her husband was in St. Paul on business and she and the children were alone.

The storm increased. The rain and wind splattered against the house. The thunder and lightning were almost continuous. The lights glowed and dimmed, sometimes leaving the house in darkness.

I noticed that the woman became more agitated as the storm worsened. She paced the floor and alternately pulled the curtains, trying to shut out the storm, and raised them to stare into the darkness.

I was seated at the dining room table writing my daily report. She sat down in a chair across from me looking driven and distraught.

"I hate storms," she said. "The things I see in them frighten me terribly, although I should be used to them by now. They certainly are moving around tonight."

I did not know who they might be, but she continued.

"People who have only the usual perceptions are fortunate. I remember the first time I realized that I could see things not visible to most other people. We were living in Pennsylvania. It was early spring and two girlfriends and I were coming home from school. Suddenly I saw great flocks of birds flying. They were all kinds and sizes. But they weren't really flying — it was as if the wind was blowing them along and they were dead.

"I told my friends about them but they couldn't see any birds. They thought I was play acting. I went home and told my mother who nodded and said, 'So you have the power, too.' She explained that it would be better not to tell others what I saw.

"Late one evening that fall, Mother and I were in our front room when we heard someone walking with a cane come slowly up our walkway. It was quite dark but I saw a shadowy figure climb our steps. The door to the vestibule opened and we heard a cane rattle into the umbrella stand. Mother opened the door but there was no one there. She started to cry and said, 'Your grandfather is dead.'

"It was true, Grandfather had died that evening.

"The following spring a neighbor boy, a good friend of mine, fell into a stone quarry and was killed. A few days after the funeral as I came along the street, I saw him sitting on the steps of his home. Then he vanished."

I was staring at the woman in amazement but she was lost in her own reverie. After a pause she spoke again.

"Then my father bought this half section with good buildings on a tax title. We soon found out why.

"It was a night like this. I had stepped outside to get some towels that had been left on the line on the back porch and as I took down the last one I glanced around and nearly fainted. A man stood in the yard in the rain. He was dressed in city clothes. The entire side of his head was crushed in. He was dead. Yet he seemed to beckon to me. I rushed into the kitchen. My mother glanced at me and nodded, 'I have seen him too,' she said.

"A few nights later one of our horses got the colic and my father stayed in the barn to care for him. After about an hour the horse got to his feet and unconcernedly began eating his hay. Father picked up his lantern, and as he turned to leave the barn the figure of the man with the crushed skull stood before him.

"My father was stunned and frightened. It was the first apparition he had ever seen. The ghost backed slowly from the barn, beckoning Father to follow. When it reached a wagon that stood in the yard it raised its hands to its head in a gesture of agony and slowly sank into the ground.

"Father came into the house, white and shaken. After he had told us what he had seen Mother said thoughtfully, 'This is no wandering spirit. He is here. His soul cannot rest and his spirit cries for help. We must dig where he disappeared and if he is there we must give him a Christian burial.'

"We had dug down only five feet when we found his remains. We buried him in our cemetery and never saw his spirit again."

The woman stopped talking. She seemed more composed and I suddenly noticed that the storm was over. There was only the sound of water dripping from the eaves and the faint rumble of thunder in the distance.

My friend's wife looked at me. "You are fortunate," she repeated, "that you cannot see what is out there in these wild storms."
— *Al Schroeder, Johnson Creek, Wisconsin*
October 1960

VISITS FROM THE DEAD

I asked who the caller was. The operator replied, "Gloria."
I then asked "Gloria who?"
She said "Gloria Aguilar."
I was dumbfounded. Gloria Aguilar, a friend of mine, had been dead for 15 years.
  — From Mary Pressey's "Gloria's Long-Distance Call," page 141

They are confused and lost. They have unfinished business. They want to say good-bye. These are the reasons, we typically assume, that spirits make an appearance among the living. But as the reports in this chapter reveal, spirits appear for numerous reasons, and sometimes no reason at all. Their visits from beyond can be frightening, soothing, and even physically dangerous.

A Vision or a Dream?

I never knew my mother, Irèn Balazs, because she died when she was 19 years of age and I was only one month old. And I hardly knew my father, Andras Balazs, either. He was the stranger who occasionally came to visit me at my grandparents' home, where I lived. Of course I knew that he was my father, but he seemed so awkward and shy in my presence, and he made me feel uncomfortable.

The spring of 1944 was the last time I saw my father. He brought me a shiny new red bike, and he took me for a ride on it. I was seven years old and loved the bike, but when my father asked for a hug after our ride, I offered a handshake instead.

"I know I'm almost a stranger to you, but you're my only child and I love you," my father told me that day. "I loved your mama, too, more than I can ever say. When the war ends, you and I will get to know each other better, I promise you that."

He never got the chance to make good on his promise, because fate intervened.

We lived in the Bacska region of Hungary in 1944. My father was in the army during World War II, and Tito and his communist partisans were soon breathing down our necks. My grandfather, Jozef Sailak, decided to move us to safer surroundings soon afterward. There was no time to notify their son-in-law of our move. Besides, we weren't quite sure where we would end up.

We finally settled down again in the upper region of Hungary, near the Austrian border. But our surroundings did not stay safe for very long. The city we were living in was bombed, and we narrowly escaped being buried alive.

From there we moved to a rural area, hoping that setting would be safer. But when the spring of 1945 arrived, so did the Russians, and Hungary was no longer a free country. In the fall of 1947, after living under the Russians for two years, we finally managed to escape into neighboring Austria.

In Austria, we joined thousands of other destitute refugees in displaced persons camps, for that is what we had became — displaced people who were without a country.

In 1951, our hopes for a better life became a reality when we were allowed to emigrate to the U.S. We boarded an old Navy ship, The U.S.S. *General Stewart*, in September of that year. It was an emotional time for us all.

"We'll never see our old homeland again," my grandfather lamented sadly as the ship pulled out of the harbor of Bremen, Germany.

"But we're on our way to America, the land of opportunity!" my grandma, Terez Sailak, added. At that moment I thought of my father and the promise he had made the last time I had seen him. Perhaps he hadn't even survived the war, and if he had survived, we had no idea where he was.

In America life was busy and good. We lived in Cleveland, Ohio. My grandparents went to work and I went to school. We never talked about my father, and I can't recall ever thinking about him.

Then, in June 1954, when I was 17 years old and had not seen my father for 10 years, something intervened on my father's behalf. It was the only psychic experience I have ever had, but it made a lasting impression that I will never forget.

One night, in the spring of that year, I had gone to bed as usual, my mind filled with plans for the coming weekend. I was going to a dance. A special boy would also be there, and sweet promise was in the air. Suddenly, a vision appeared at the foot of my bed. It was a beautiful young woman with long, flowing blond hair, wearing a sad expression on her strangely familiar face. I sat up and stared at her, not at all frightened, for though I had never met her, I knew who she was. She was my mother.

"You must get in touch with your father. He is very worried about you, because he doesn't know what's happened to you. He needs to know that you're alive and well so he can go on with his life in peace. You must do this very soon," she said in a voice that was just above a whisper. Then she was gone.

I sat there in my bed and began to cry. I cried for never having known her, and I cried for my father and all the sadness I had caused him. Finally, my grandmother must have heard me, because she came into my room to ask what was wrong. I told her about the vision. Or had it been a dream? I was not quite sure.

Grandma began to cry, too. My mother had been her only child, and though we hadn't talked about her much lately, I always knew her passing had left my grandmother with a permanent heartache.

The following morning, my grandparents wrote a letter to a relative who still lived in the old country, inquiring about my father. Three weeks later I received a jubilant letter from him.

"Though we're separated by a great ocean now, I'm so happy to know that you're well, my dear child. Never forget that I will always love you. And I will always love your mama, too," my father wrote in that first letter. And when I answered his letter, I told him about the vision. I told him that my mama still loved him too, even from beyond the grave. I realized that I loved my father and that I was not as indifferent as I used to believe that I was.

— *Renie Burghardt, Doniphan, Missouri*
April 1995

Gloria's Long-Distance Call

For many years I received intermittent phone calls from a caller who would not respond when I answered. I was puzzled at first, and then annoyed that the caller would be so timid or perhaps obnoxious enough to try to disturb my peace of mind.

In November 1996, after I returned home from a stimulating concert, my phone rang. When I answered it, I was asked by the operator whether I would accept a collect call. I asked who the caller was. The operator replied, "Gloria."

I then asked, "Gloria who?"

She said, "Gloria Aguilar."

I was dumbfounded. Gloria Aguilar, a friend of mine, had been dead for 15 years. I told the operator I would accept the call and proceeded to listen. Gloria did not speak to me. I waited and waited, saying "hello, hello" over and over into the telephone. There was no answer. When I hung up the phone I was in shock — Gloria had been pushed down a flight of stairs by a thief who stole her purse.

She had hit her head against the cement railing and died instantly.

The next morning at 10:00 A.M., the phone rang. It rang again at 11:00 A.M. but there was no response. By this time I was sure that Gloria was trying to reach me and so I picked up my pendulum and asked, "Gloria, are you here?" After a pause the pendulum swung with an unexpected drive toward me, indicating that she was.

I asked her, "Do you know that you are dead, that you were pushed down some stairs and died instantly?"

There was no response. My pendulum would not move at all.

I then implored her to go toward the light, to release herself from the earthly plane. I am sure she followed my advice; I no longer get the strange, mysterious phone calls.

— *Mary Pressey, Forest Hills, New York*
August 1997

Uncle Erick

In April 1982, I had finished compiling my late mother's side of our family tree, but I lacked vital statistics and a photograph of her closest relative and only sibling — a deceased bachelor named Erick Soronen whom I had never met.

A disagreement over their father's will led my mother to refuse to have anything further to do with the Soronen side of her family. She had been left the sum of one dollar while Uncle Erick inherited the 160-acre family farm near Menahga in central Minnesota. Mother let it be known, in no uncertain terms, that when she died, Uncle Erick would not be included in her obituary, nor would he be under obligation to attend her funeral. His name was rarely mentioned.

As I knew virtually nothing about Uncle Erick and because I had no tangible leads to follow, I placed ads in *The Farmer* magazine and the Minnesota *New York Mills Herald*, asking for anyone with knowledge and photographs of the Soronen family, former pioneer settlers from the Menahga-New York Mills area, to contact me at my home in Minneapolis.

Within three weeks I received a letter from one of Uncle Erick's neighbors with information copied from a World War I veteran's book concerning his army service in France.

Several days later, while I was watching a late movie on television, I had a sudden strong urge to type an individual genealogy sheet on Uncle Erick based on his army data. After finishing the sheet, I returned to watch television. I must have dozed off on the davenport. Around midnight, I was awakened by loud, echoing raps coming from the kitchen. I switched on the ceiling lamp and went to answer the door, thinking it would be Hildirig Bergquist, my next door neighbor, who was helping me translate family data from Swedish to English.

Because I was half-awake, I didn't ask who it was. I was surprised to see an unknown man wearing a dark jacket and a 1940s style snap-brim fedora that hid part of his face. He appeared to be looking for a lost object on the floor. After I asked if I could be of assistance, he slowly raised his head.

At that instant I saw an expression of hostility directed toward me. The hairs on my arms and neck stood up and bone-chilling shivers passed through my body. Without saying a word or making a gesture, the stranger vanished. He did not dissolve into a wisp of mist or float away; his disappearance was comparable to erasing a drawing from a blackboard with one large swipe.

After several sleepless nights I no longer thought about my encounter with the stranger. Then, a few days later, I received in the mail a small snapshot of a man identical in appearance to my unknown nocturnal caller. A letter enclosed with the snapshot identified the man as my estranged Uncle Erick.

Apparently Uncle Erick had let me know that he didn't want to be included in the family genealogy. This experience strengthened my belief both in survival after death and in other facets of psychic phenomena.

— *Glen Kartin, Duluth, Minnesota*
June 1995

Billy Comes Back

An event took place on Christmas Eve, 1908, in the tiny farm village of Ethelbert, Manitoba, that was memorable — at least to the youngest members of my grandmother's family.

The area was settled by Ukrainians in the 1890s. Farms in all directions were owned by people who came primarily from Galicia, in what was then Austria-Hungary. They were hard-working folk who barely scratched a living from the stony ground.

They told a wealth of legends and stories, and a strong belief in the supernatural was common. Faith in the afterlife was as certain and inevitable as we believe that if today is Sunday tomorrow must be Monday. These beliefs had a steadying influence on people.

On Christmas Eve, my grandmother, Pearl Zabinski, was busily setting the large homemade table in her family's chilly, seldom-used dining room in preparation for the next day's Christmas dinner, when neighbors would come by horse from miles around.

Some of the children were helping their mama — my grandmother — get the room ready. As is the Ukrainian tradition, there was hay on the floor and the best heads of wheat were lightly spread under the tablecloth. The table was set with 12 traditional meatless dishes. Each dish represented one of Christ's apostles.

The table was set against the wall and an oil lamp glowed, showing off the treasures of the new settlers, which were brought out and used only on these high holidays. The children's mother had just finished saying that she hoped everybody would come, when eight-year-old Ann yelled out, "Billy has come! Billy has come!"

There, on the floor beneath the table, illuminated by the dull glow of the table lamp, stood a two-year-old figure dressed in white, as their brother Billy had been dressed when he was buried in the village cemetery two years before. All the children were jumping about with delight. Billy had come home at last!

But his mother could see nothing. The smiling figure held his little hands clasped together, just as he had when he was buried. The vision lasted a considerable time before it gradually began to fade, leaving an aural light under the table. All the children thought it was the best Christmas ever, but it was some time before their mother regained her composure.

This story was told at many Christmas Eves up to the present, celebrating an event that took place 87 years ago.

There is an unshakable belief in our extended family that death opens a door into an unknown world. Billy's visit was something of a cultural lesson in Ukrainian beliefs for our little farming town. Years later, mama, now a grandmother herself and very advanced in years, still expressed sorrow that she saw nothing. But the children of the house were treated to a Christmas Eve visit from the vast beyond by their brother Billy.

— *Walter Krivda, Manitoba, Canada*
June 1995

The Boss from Beyond

In the spring of 1955, I was working for an international trading firm run by three brothers. The oldest brother, Franklin, had leukemia. Though he grew weaker and weaker as his illness progressed, he continued to come to the office.

Franklin was a tall, gray-haired gentleman, heavyset, impeccably dressed and groomed, always courteous, and somewhat formal in his manner.

The business was his life. He never took a vacation and his only trips had been business trips. When at last he was physically unable to come to work, the other brothers brought copies of all the days' correspondence, which he kept under his pillow.

Franklin died. I went to his funeral on Sunday. On Monday, the firm was open for business as usual. I opened the office as usual at 8:30 A.M. The other offices on the floor were still dark at that hour, and it always seemed to me as if I worked in the only office in an empty building.

As I inserted my key into the door, I heard heavy footsteps inside. Jack, the middle brother, had spoken about having a safe installed, so I assumed that he had arranged to have the work done before the business day.

But as I opened the door, I was surprised to find that the office was still dark. I switched on the lights. I was alone. At the teletype along the wall was the usual sheet of cables extending to the floor. I acknowledged the cables, pulled off the sheet, and took it to my desk in the outer office. There I sat down with my cup of coffee and the Boe Code Book to decipher the messages. I liked this part of the day; it was like solving puzzles.

Just as I settled down, I heard a loud rustle of papers in the inner office, where Jack would soon occupy Franklin's swivel chair.

"The correspondence must be blowing all over the floor!" I thought. I hurried past the glass door to find the letters neatly piled on the desk with a paperweight over them. The window was closed.

I went back to my desk, my coffee and the Boe Code. I had hardly sat down when the swivel chair creaked loudly, with another rustling of paper. When I stood, I could see the inner office. The sounds ceased and nothing moved.

I sat down again. At once, the creak and the rustle sounded clearly. Again, I stood, and again all noises stopped.

I sipped my coffee and read the cables. The creaking and rustling resumed.

"If Franklin wants to see the correspondence, let him," I decided. I knew he had no reason to harm me and I had none to disturb him, so we both quietly went on with our work until 9:00 A.M. when the office day began and my colleague, Sylvia, arrived.

"I dreamed Franklin came back to the office," she said.

"He did," I told her. We talked it over and decided not to mention it to the surviving brothers, not knowing how they might react. We never told anyone about the episode, until now.

— *Charlotte A. Kellar, New York, New York*
August 1997

A Brother's Revenge

Jim Daniel of Logan County, West Virginia, joined the Army early in 1917 and was among the first of the American Expeditionary Force to arrive in France. His letters at first came regularly to his girlfriend, Darlene Mastin, then they stopped entirely.

Darlene continued to write for some time, not knowing that Will Daniel, Jim's older brother, was intercepting their mail — for Will also was in love with Darlene. He finally faked a telegram, stating Jimmy had been killed in action. Showing Darlene this telegram, he played so cleverly on her anguish that she agreed to marry him.

Will and Darlene were married in October and all went well until Christmas Eve, 1917. Darlene, who was preparing supper, heard the front door open and recognized Jim Daniel's voice saying to her husband, Will, who was sitting in the living room: "I know what you have done to Darlene and me and I have come to kill you as you deserve." Darlene knew that mountain people weren't in the habit of speaking without meaning what they said. She realized that Will either had made a mistake or deliberately had lied to her about Jim's death, as Jim was suddenly back home — and very much alive.

Darlene heard a shot and ran into the front room just in time to see a man in uniform go out the door. Will lay dead on the living room floor, a hole in his forehead and a look of disbelief in his dulling eyes.

How long Darlene stood rooted to the spot, staring down at her dead husband, she never remembered. A brisk rapping on the front door brought her back to reality. Opening the door she saw a boy with a telegram. It was from the War Department and read: "To William Daniel: Regret to inform you that on December 21, 1917, your brother, James Daniel, was killed in action in Germany."

Will's murderer never was apprehended. There was no trace of anyone, other than the Western Union boy, ever having been to the Daniel home that night. No gun ever was found and it was proven that Will Daniel never had owned a gun. Darlene insisted that the ghost of the wronged brother had returned after death and done the killing.

— *Lonnie E. Legge, Lewisburg, West Virginia*
August 1958

Ghost of My Great-Great Grandfather

Twenty years ago, after the death of my father, Glen A. Hyde, I decided to do something as a memorial and I hit upon the idea of tracing our family tree.

One summer evening in 1985, I was going to the W&J Library in Washington, Pennsylvania, to do some research. It was dark and raining very hard as I came around a bend. There by the wayside stood an old man, dripping wet. Usually I do not pick up hitchhikers, but he looked harmless. He nodded when I asked him if he wanted a ride into town.

I stole a glance at him. He seemed to be about 90 years old. His hair and goatee were white. He wore old-fashioned pinstriped trousers and a black vest with a watch fob chain across the lapels. He also had on a black swallowtail coat. I thought perhaps he was an old-time preacher in the back hills.

He asked me where I was going. "Peculiar," I thought, "I should be asking him." I said I was going to the library to find some data on land grants in Somerset and Bedford County, Pennsylvania. He told me to look on the third shelf, the red books, fourth volume, page 289, where I would find the information I needed. "Have you been here before?" I asked.

"Yes and no," he replied.

I thought that was an odd answer, and I told him I would let him off in town, where he could catch a bus. He said he didn't need one, so I thought someone was picking him up.

When I looked back at him, he was gone. I had not heard or seen the car door open or shut, nor felt the rain coming in. He had not said good-bye. He just vanished into thin air. There was still an indentation in the seat where he had been sitting. Oddly, it was dry, even though he had been dripping wet when he got in. There was no sign of him on the road, either in front of or behind me.

I did not think of him again until I spoke to my aunt, who was doing some research with me. She gave me some photos that her mother had left in the attic. After Christmas I decided to look at them. There before my astonished eyes was a picture of the old man

I had seen in my car. In the photo, the old man was sitting in front of a fence with a house in the background. He had on the same outfit that the man who had ridden in my car wore — pinstriped trousers, a watch fob chain across his vest, and a swallowtail coat. He had white hair and a goatee. I turned the picture over. Written on it was, "This is your great-great-grandfather, Johnathan Hyde, Civil War veteran."

I called my aunt and excitedly told her my incredible story, but I don't know whether she believed me or not. Wilder yet, I told her, this man had been three-dimensional. He had talked to me. There was an indention in the seat where he had sat, just as a normal person would create.

I did find the facts I wanted just where he said I would. It was a very unusual experience. I had been talking with the ghost of my great-great-grandfather, Johnathan Hyde, a Civil War veteran dead over 100 years. Strange but true!

— *Marilyn Vanistendael, Canonsburg, Pennsylvania*
May 1995

Taken by Aunt Elsie

My aunt Elsie was the oldest sister of my father, Daniel Aragon. She had raised him and her frequent visits to our house in Trinidad, Colorado, were proof of her strong affection for him.

Aunt Elsie was a proud, arrogant woman and at times I resented her overbearing ways. I especially resented the way she always said, "I'll never leave this world without taking my brother Dan with me." The conviction with which she said this made me feel strangely helpless, for I too loved Father.

Her visit in the summer of 1941 lasted longer than usual and I was relieved when finally she returned to her home in New Mexico.

A few weeks later Father suddenly fell ill. The doctor said it was nothing serious and that Father should be up and around again in a few days. He was wrong, however, for three days later Father died.

We had no telephone and after the first shock of Father's death I was sent to a neighbor's house to call Aunt Elsie and tell her of our loss. A strange woman answered Aunt Elsie's phone and informed me that she was the landlady. When I told her who I was she gasped with relief. "I've been trying to reach you all day! " she cried. "Your Aunt Elsie passed away at eight o'clock this morning."

I hung up the phone in a daze. Father had died at nine o'clock.
— *Mrs. Charles Chaves*
October 1958

The Guiding Spirit

It was December 17, 1950. In Catron County, New Mexico, snow had fallen all day and drifted against the house almost to the tops of the low windows. My husband had gone to a neighboring ranch on business, so the children and I were alone. I knew my husband could not return until snowplows cleared the roads, but there was no need to worry. We were plentifully supplied with food and wood.

After the children had gone to bed. I sat up knitting by the light of a kerosene lamp.

We lived more than 100 miles from a city, hospital, or railroad. I was the only nurse for miles, and the nearest doctor was 20 miles distant. Consequently people often came to me for help, and I was not surprised when I heard a knock on the door. There I found a small dark woman carrying a lantern. She was wrapped in a dark gray blanket and spoke in broken English: "Señora, you please to come with me. My daughter, Ignasia, has her baby tonight."

I asked the woman to come in and hurriedly got ready to face the storm. I woke my eldest daughter and told her not to look for me until perhaps late the next day. Soon the woman and I were struggling along in the dark and the snow — at least I was struggling; my companion flitted ahead of me like a shadow.

At last we arrived, breathless, at a small cabin. Entering, I saw a young Mexican woman already in labor. I scrubbed and got busy.

Hours later a baby boy was born. His lusty wail filled the cabin.

I turned and said, "Madre, here is a fine grandson" — but the little, dark woman had vanished! She did not return.

Next day, the snow quit falling and the young woman's husband returned from town with supplies. He was amazed to find himself a father and still more surprised to find me there.

"Nurse, how did you know?" he asked me.

When I told him his wife's mother had come for me, his face went white and he crossed himself.

"No! That cannot be. My wife's mother died 19 years ago last night — when Ignasia was born!"

— M. M., Auburn, California
November 1954

A Chat with the Dead

In November 1910, my sister Ellen fell so seriously ill that we feared for her life. As we were unable to obtain a nurse, a cousin and I took care of her. My cousin took the night watch and I stayed with Ellen during the day.

Across the street lived a couple by the name of Clark who were close friends of ours. The husband, Steve, also was very ill at the time and we had been very careful to keep this knowledge from Ellen. No one entered her room except the doctor, my cousin and myself. In fact, she had been in a sort of coma for some time and had not been much aware of anything.

Early one morning, I was sitting beside Ellen's bed when she began to talk in a low tone with her eyes closed. She said, "Hello, Steve, what are you doing here?" I heard no reply but Ellen seemed to, for she said, "I am sorry you have to go, Steve. We will miss you."

She then carried on a conversation of which I heard her side only; she answered questions and asked some. Whoever she was talking to seemed to urge her to go with him, for she finally said, "No. Steve, I would like to go — it sounds lovely. But I can't leave my children; they are little and they need me. Goodbye, Steve, and good luck." Then she gave a sigh and seemed to sleep.

A short time later she opened her eyes and looked at me with the first sign of recognition I had seen for days. She asked, "Why didn't you tell me Steve was dead?"

I stammered, "Why, he isn't dead — what made you think that?" We had not had any news from outside the house that day.

Ellen said calmly, "I know he is dead; he was here a few minutes ago, talking to me. He said he had to go away, and he wanted me to go too. I would like to have gone, but I couldn't leave the children."

I said desperately, "Why, Ellen, you have been dreaming. You were asleep." She said, "No, I wasn't asleep; I saw him. He sat right here on the foot of the bed and talked to me. He was wearing his brown suit with a pink carnation in his buttonhole. He looked wonderful."

I called the doctor and he came and talked to us. He had been over at the Clark house across the street. Steve had died during the night. He was laid out in a brown suit with a pink carnation in his buttonhole, slipped in by his wife.

Ellen recovered and lived a long and useful life, but if I live to be 100 I never will forget her chat with the dead.

— *Mary A. Davis, San Francisco, California*
August 1958

I Saw My Father in the Mirror

In the spring of 1949 I experienced what I believe was a contact with the spirit world. I was sitting in my grandmother's living room one day, quietly chatting about family affairs.

She sat on the sofa facing me. Behind her on the wall was a wide mirror. Her back was to the mirror, but I could look directly into it. As we spoke I glanced into the mirror and saw my face change. My grandmother stopped talking for a few seconds, then finished the discussion.

My face had seemed to change shape into the face of my father, who had died two years before. I decided not to mention what I had seen to my grandmother; she was a very religious, down-to-earth person who might not approve of what I saw. Then, after a silence, she said, "Do you know, I never thought you looked much like your father. I always thought that you resembled your mother's people. But just for a minute there, I saw a look on your face that was exactly like your father's. It was uncanny."

I knew then that she had seen for herself what I had seen in the mirror. We talked about him in a warm, loving way, both of us regretting that he had left us too soon. Years later, I told a medium what had happened. She said that the phenomenon was called transmigration. She said that my father wanted to make his mother think of him and send his love to both of us. He was a very loving, sentimental person when he was on this plane, so I believe transmigration explains what happened that day. I know that my grandmother and I both saw it.

— *Virginia McCauley, Wellsville, Ohio*
January 1997

To Watch Over Her

I n 1913, my sister lay ill with scarlet fever. The doctor had told us it was not serious, that she would be up and around in a couple of weeks.

My boys were away at summer camp and I was staying with Sis to take care of her and her 11-month-old baby, Lura Luceal.

Everything was going well until one day when I heard her sobbing.

"Sis, what is the matter?" I asked. "The doctor said you will be okay in a few days. Why cry now?"

"The doctor is wrong, I know," she sobbed. "I don't really mind so much for myself, but why do I have to leave Lura? She is so tiny. What will happen to her?"

Sometime later, after she had stopped crying, she said, "If only I could watch over her until she grows up. Do you suppose God might let me do that?"

A week later Sis died. She had tuberculosis along with the scarlet fever and at that time there were no wonder drugs to combat such a combination. Once she started hemorrhaging it was all over.

My brother-in-law remarried when Lura was two years old, and although I begged him to let her stay and grow up as a sister for my two boys, he refused. They moved away from me and it nearly broke my heart.

Years passed and the stepmother didn't want Lura to know anything about her mother's folks. All our gifts and letters were returned to us unopened. There was nothing we could do about it.

Then my mother died and left my sister's share of the estate to Lura. It was necessary for her to make a trip west to claim the inheritance.

It was a shock to meet Lura at the depot. She looked just like her mother.

As old folks will do, I showed Lura old family pictures, and she seemed to enjoy going over them with me. All of a sudden she selected one and held it up. "Who is this? Who is this lady?"

"My dear, don't you know? Have you never seen a picture of your mother?" I asked, shocked.

"Oh, no," she said. "Mom wouldn't let me see any. And the things she told me about my mother were horrid. But this lady is beautiful."

"Your mother was beautiful and so good!" I said, and spent the rest of the afternoon telling her about her mother.

"Tell me," she said, "how my mother was buried."

I explained that her mother had been buried in her long white wedding dress.

"And her hair? Was it long and brown? Was it flecked with gold and ever so gently curly?"

"Yes, child, why do you ask?" I answered.

"Oh," she cried, her eyes shining through the tears. "Now I know who the lovely lady was that came to visit me. Once when I was very unhappy, I prayed and prayed. It was just after I had learned to read. The Bible stories I read on the sly intrigued me. And a lady dressed in a long white dress and with long brown hair came to me and smiled and said, 'Be patient, baby; be patient.'

"Oh, Aunt Peggy, how I loved that lady. Every time I grew unhappy she would visit. Sometimes she would just smile. Sometimes she would just nod her head as if to say, 'You are doing okay.' And I always felt better and would sing while I worked all the next day."

I told her how her mother had prayed to be allowed to watch over her until she grew up.

"Oh, Aunt Peggy," Lura said sadly. "I am almost sad I have grown up. She doesn't visit me anymore."

— *Val Spiers, Boise, Idaho*
October 1960

Death Is But a Shadow

When my father's physical condition deteriorated, we could only wait. The night before his death, I was with him and saw his soul moving away. I kissed his head, wished him well on his journey, and left knowing that tomorrow would be an end and a beginning for all who loved him.

The next morning I was called to identify his body and collect his personal belongings. When I entered the room, I was overwhelmed. There was only a shell — no warmth, no substance. His body was empty of that life-giving individual essence. I returned home shaken, but tried to be strong for my family. My son Karl, four, awoke just before the call and had come downstairs to tell my husband about a dream.

"Grandpa says he has to go away now," Karl said sleepily, rubbing blurry eyes. "But he says not to worry, he feels much better now."

Then he hugged his father and continued with his morning routine. Had he heard my husband and me talking, or had my father's namesake experienced a spiritual encounter? I believe that children are more open to these experiences because of their simple trust.

Later that day when my sister called, Karl volunteered, "Oh, Aunt Kathy, don't be sad. Grandpa's okay, and he's not sick any more."

For the first year after my father's death, Karl drew pictures of his grandfather by himself. Once when I asked him, he said that Grandpa was in his dreams last night, saying that "he likes me and wants to play with my toys."

My father had been so ill that he couldn't play with Karl. The final year, his discomfort had been so intolerable that mostly he yelled at Karl from frustration. In one brief visit, he had healed those wounds and given Karl a beautiful memory.

I always missed Dad most between Thanksgiving and Christmas, since he always enjoyed playing a bountiful Santa. On December 15, 1992, he showed up again. Earlier that week I'd had impressions of someone looking over my shoulder as I worked on a forthcoming book.

For Karl, who had reached a semi-fearful age, this wasn't as pleasant an experience as it had been in the past. He came running downstairs sobbing, "Mommy, my grandpa died! Why did he have to go away?"

"He was very sick and in pain, and needed to rest," I said, trying to sooth him and hold him close.

"He was with me in bed. I thought he was Santa Claus," Karl said.

"Grandpa didn't mean to scare you or make you sad. He just loves you and probably wanted to make sure you were okay," I explained. "Did he tell you anything?"

"Just to be good," Karl said.

So that was it. This had been a year of struggle with Karl, who was willfully exerting his independence. Dad must have sensed my frustration and tried to help.

I told Karl that his grandpa loved him and wanted what was best, and that he should wish his grandpa happy holidays and tell him that he loved him. Karl sighed, rubbed his eyes and slowly went back upstairs to sleep without incident.

I looked around at my home. A 10-foot tree covered with Victorian ornaments blinked merrily. I knew that Dad would be here every Christmas. More importantly, he would be with Karl.

Death was only a shadow — and where there is a shadow, there must also be bountiful light!

— *Trish Telesco, Buffalo, New York*
December 1993

My Mystery Angel

In 1990, I became pregnant with my second child. I was happy and excited, but four months into the pregnancy problems started, because I was diagnosed with placenta abruptio.

For a month and a half, I was in and out of St. Mary's Hospital in Stoughton, Wisconsin. Then, very suddenly, I went into labor. They had to let the baby come because there were a lot of other complications, and my life would have been in danger if the baby wasn't born.

I gave birth to a baby girl who weighed one pound and one ounce. We named her Jessica. She was much too small and undeveloped to survive, and passed away two hours after her birth.

Several years later, I started babysitting for my nephew, Seth. He would spend the night at my house because my sister, Chris, worked nights.

Everything was fine for a while, but one night I was awakened by my daughter Melissa's cries, so I got up to check on her. I got Melissa quieted down and headed back to my room.

Suddenly I saw a young child run past the couch and into the kitchen.

I automatically assumed it was Seth. I called to him, but the child kept going. I followed him into the kitchen, still calling out Seth's name, but the child was gone. I thought he was hiding from me, so I looked under the table, by the side of the refrigerator, and next to the washing machine.

Still unable to find him, I decided to check the couch. There Seth was, still sleeping soundly. I became frightened and hurried back to bed with my husband, Robert Foote, Jr. After a while, I fell asleep.

Almost a week later I was again awakened by Melissa's cries. I went to her room and gave her a pacifier before laying her down again in her bed. As I was coming out of her room, I saw the same young child by the couch where Seth was sleeping.

But this time I saw that the child was a girl with long curls. She was about the size of an 18-month old infant, the same age my daughter would have been had she lived. I stopped dead in my tracks when I saw her. I was shocked.

She ran into the kitchen again. I didn't follow her this time, because as I stood there I could see my nephew asleep on the couch.

I went to my room and woke up my husband to tell him what happened. He thought I was crazy, but I know what I saw. Every night after that I slept with the light on.

I no longer saw her, and had forgotten about her until two months later, when my nephew passed away very suddenly after he fell off his horse and was stepped on. He died almost instantly of a ruptured spleen.

After that I started to wonder about the little girl again. I questioned what she was doing at my house, near the couch where my nephew had slept, and if she could have been Jessica, waiting to lead Seth on his way?

A year and a half later, my grandma, Eleanor, who lived downstairs in the same house, woke up from a nap and was startled by a young girl running past her. When she realized that the little girl was nowhere to be found, she shrugged it off as a bad dream.

In December 1992, my grandma passed away from a blood clot. She had seen the girl just five months before she died.

I don't really know why that little girl was there or who she was, but I would like to believe that it was Jessica. Maybe she was a guardian angel sent there to lead them on their way.

— *Jackie Foote, Stoughton, Wisconsin*
December 1993

I Never Heard the Train That Killed Me

C ome on, Sam, while we have a few hours to kill, let's look up that spiritualist, Mrs. Saidie Blake. Let's see if she can call up some spirit to pass the time of day with."

Young Edward Giles spoke to his companion, Sam Austin. The young men were from Durbin, West Virginia, but were stranded between trains at Huntington. This was back in 1905 when we used to laugh about such things as automobiles, airplanes, moving pictures, and radios. Atom bombs and space travel were undreamed of.

A few inquiries disclosed that this woman — who was credited by many people with supernatural powers — lived across the Ohio River, at Chesapeake, Ohio, and could only be reached by the ferry. The ferry landing was up the railroad track.

"I'll go along with you," said Sam, "but I don't put much stock in anything to do with supernatural powers, especially calling up the dead."

"You ought to be ashamed of yourself, Sam, disputing the Bible which plainly states in First Samuel that the Witch of Endor called up Samuel for King Saul to interview."

"Well," replied Sam, smiling, "those old timers could do things that are impossible today."

"There you go again, disputing the good book," Ed replied.

They continued their good-natured banter until they were near the ferry landing. Then Sam said, "I'll prove my point by sitting here on the track until you return. Tell the old lady you want to talk to your friend, Sam Austin. When a voice answers you will know what a fake she really is."

"All right," Ed replied hesitantly. "I'll take you up on that. Maybe we'll both learn something."

Ed boarded the ferry, leaving his friend seated on the end of a railway tie just above the ferry landing.

By the time he got across the river and located the spiritualist's home nearly an hour had elapsed. He was lucky that she could see him right away without an appointment. She readily agreed to try to contact his friend.

Seated in a chair, holding a long tin horn in his arms, Ed watched the old lady drop off into a self-induced hypnotic sleep. The horn soon became very heavy in his hands. Then a voice he instantly recognized as his friend's seemed to issue from the horn, saying, "Well, Ed, I am actually here."

"Sure I know," Ed exclaimed. "Still sitting across the river on the railroad track."

"No," the voice answered soberly. "I'll explain to you! Last night, as you know, we did not get much sleep and, while watching the ferry cross the river, I must have dozed off. I never even heard the train that struck and killed me. Doesn't the Bible also say something about, 'in the midst of life we are in death?' Ed, you certainly have taught me a lesson, but at what a price. Farewell."

The voice died away as the medium came out of her trance and asked Ed what had happened. He told her curtly, adding, "That just goes to show that you don't know what you are talking about. My friend is very much alive, sitting across the river, waiting on me."

"I wouldn't say that," the medium answered wearily.

Ed left the house quickly, vowing never to be misled into trying to talk to the dead again. As he boarded the ferry he could see a rather large crowd collected on the other side of the river. He asked the ferry attendant what was going on.

"Some fellow went to sleep on the railroad track and a train ran over him," the man replied.

"Did it kill him?" Ed whispered.

"Yes, instantly! He's already been taken to the Huntington morgue until further identification is made."

With leaden heart Ed found the morgue and asked to see the train victim. When the sheet-shrouded figure was uncovered he looked into his friend's staring eyes. But his usual sardonic grin was replaced by a tranquil smile.

He was so startled he involuntarily exclaimed, "Sam! It was just a coincidence?"

As if from a great distance, a low, firm voice — which Ed later swore was his friend's — seemed to say, "I wouldn't say that!"

— *Lonnie E. Legge, Lewisburg, West Virginia*
October 1959

Olga Keeps Her Promise

I was raised in the atmosphere of extreme materialism that dominated the 1920s. From this environment I drew two conclusions about the "dead" — either they were completely extinct, or they existed in some unknown, inaccessible state. In Sunday school, I embarrassed my teachers with questions about the hereafter. I read my Bible avidly, hoping to find support for the theory of survival, but I was not satisfied. It was not until I entered high school that all doubt was erased from my mind.

In the fall of 1925, when I was 16, I left my farm home to board in Chanute, Kansas, where the high school was located. Here I met Olga Hanson. She seemed an ordinary farm girl like myself. She was tall and blonde, of Nordic descent, and had a rather serious nature. We shared a number of classes, the most important being English, for it was here we found a common interest in the study of literature.

One day we were discussing the current assignment, which happened to be ghost stories. It led to an intimate conversation between us as to the possibility of the dead returning in the form of apparitions or in some other way. Finally, we decided to prove the thing in the only possible way — by promising each other that the first to die would return and tell the surviving one all about it. The pact was sealed, after which the subject was never mentioned again between us. I put it away somewhere in the back of my mind for the rest of the school year.

Once school let out for the summer vacation, I had no further communication with Olga because our farm homes were miles apart. In June 1926, I had a remarkable experience. I retired rather late, and it seemed I had just dozed off when I found myself walking along a familiar street in Chanute. Olga was with me.

Olga was more serious than usual but looked quite natural as we sauntered along arm in arm. Then she said, "I've come back to keep my promise!"

Her tone was quiet, to prevent startling me, I think. I turned to her unbelievingly. She seemed just the same as always. There was something a bit more profound about her manner, perhaps, but otherwise she seemed perfectly real.

"What do you mean, Olga?" I asked.

"Don't you remember our promise to each other?" she questioned. "I am dead! I have come back to tell you."

"No, no," I cried. "You can't be dead! Why, you are here walking along beside me. You look so well!" I puzzled over her words, yet I knew she spoke the truth.

Olga was patient, but at last she seemed to think that nothing short of a shock would make me understand. "Look at me!" she said. "I am dead; I died today!" Then an unearthly expression came over her countenance, turning it from youthful health to a cold pallor! Her eyes lost all expression and her hands were chill to the touch.

This alarmed and horrified me, but when I looked again she was her old familiar self.

"Now you know," she said softly. "I am dead! I cannot tell you what it is like, for it is not permitted, except to say that everything is all right. Never be afraid to die! Everything is all right!"

Just as I was about to question her further, there was a change. I cannot explain it. One moment I was with Olga, the next I was wide awake in my own bed! It wasn't like waking from a dream, slowly and drowsily. This was instantaneous! I called to my mother immediately and told her everything. A cold sweat covered my body, and I'm afraid I was very upset. Mother tried to convince me I had had a nightmare, but I felt that something awful had happened to Olga and nothing could convince me to the contrary! I didn't sleep much the rest of the night.

Daylight dispelled some of my fears, until later in the day when I went out to get the mail. The daily paper always came a day late on the rural route. When I looked on the front page, my "dream" came back to me with startling clarity!

These words jumped out at me: "Girl Drowns in Neosho River." Hurriedly, I read how Olga Hanson had gone with her family for an outing on the river. Olga's young sister, Rose, got caught in the swift undertow and was sucked beneath the river's surface. Olga swam after her and managed to get the child to safety, only to be drawn under the swirling water herself. Though others plunged to the rescue, it was too late. Olga had saved her sister at the price of her own life.

The fact that the newspaper had been published the preceding evening but not delivered until the next day, and that my dream occurred the night of the accident cannot be a coincidence. I believe Olga came back to keep her promise!

— Rosalind John
April 1955

The Kindly Priest

My high school in Cleveland, Ohio, overlooked Lake Erie. The playing field ended at a cliff with a 50-foot drop into the water. That's where I stood, ready to jump and end my miserable adolescent existence.

Suddenly, a strong arm pulled me away from the edge and whirled me around. I faced an old, frail-looking priest who asked, "Why would you kill yourself?" The last person I wanted to tell was a priest, yet his firm, kind eyes told me I'd find a compassionate ear.

All during that fall of 1967, mysterious nocturnal visitations had occurred in my room. A young man would sit on my bed, asking what I was doing in his room. My ship models would fly about, missing my head by inches. My parents didn't believe me, even though they knew that the son of the previous owner had died unexpectedly in that room. They suggested that I seek the advice of a priest at my high school.

What I received from the young cleric instead was admonishment for being a wicked child who drew the devil's work to me. Penitence and prayer were the answers, he said. He was wrong. The phenomenon continued, and I sank into a deep, self-deprecating depression.

I was afraid to tell anyone. Certain that my sinful nature had brought this upon me, I resolved that I was powerless, except to give Satan what he wanted — my life.

The old priest listened carefully to every word. As I spoke, I made myself remember the face of the only human who would listen unconditionally to my problem.

The priest finally spoke: "I have been a priest far too long not to know there's a world beyond our own feeble understanding, my son. The spirit who troubles you doesn't know he's dead. Tell him to go to the light, and in three days he'll be gone."

"Yes, Father," I nodded. I turned toward the lake and remarked, "I'd be dead by now if not for you, Father."

No answer came. I turned to see that he had traversed some distance toward the Marianist House.

"Go to the light," I heard his voice call out.

I took his advice and he was right. In three days the apparitions ceased and I found peace and a new perspective on life.

Four years later, I chanced to visit the Marianist House on business. On the vestibule wall hung a picture of the kindly priest who had saved my life and my soul. The plaque read: "Born 1855. Died 1930."

I have learned that God is a God of love unencumbered by human doctrine and that the greatest "devil" is a person's fear. I have devoted a great deal of time to learning about otherworldly things, searching within and trying to apply them to my life. I still marvel at the power of God every time I realize that on that fateful day, the old priest was able to save two souls at once.

— *William W. Casciato, Woodbridge, Virginia*
July 1993

OUT-OF-BODY EXPERIENCES

Suddenly, I found my conscious mind slightly above the trees. I was viewing my body on the ground.
— *From Freddie Booker's "I Met the Great Spirit," page 171*

Ancient Hindu teachings described three bodies that each person possesses — physical, subtle and causal — and held that the subtle body could leave and reenter the physical body. Similar ancient Egyptian beliefs said that the Ka, an ethereal copy of the corporeal body, could also travel in the physical world. Documented research in out-of-body travel would have to wait until the 1920s, when *The Occult Review* published articles by British researcher Hugh Callaway (author of *Astral Projection,* 1939), and Americans Sylvan Muldoon and Hereward Carrington published *The Projection of the Astral Body* (1929).

Since then, numerous experts have conducted thousands of experiments designed to support or refute the testimony of people like Freddie Booker. Only those who have had out-of-body experiences themselves, however, have the evidence necessary to make the distinction between hallucination, dreaming, and true astral projection.

A Cry in the Night

John Matthews yawned and got up to turn off the television while his wife Peg picked up coffee cups and ash trays. It was 1:30 A.M. on a cold January night in 1964.

As he noted the time he heard an odd sound the voice of a young child crying, "Mommy, Daddy ...."

Who could it be? Their own four-year-old had been upstairs asleep for hours. The voice seemed to be coming from somewhere down the block, moving closer until they heard it in front of their house. John glanced at Peg standing in the kitchen doorway, cups in her hands.

The voice now went on, past the house, still calling, "Mommy, Daddy ...." John went to the window and looked out. He saw light snow covering the ground, the houses across the street, stars shining in the sky.

"What do you see?" Peg asked.

"Nothing."

The voice grew fainter and then they heard it no longer.

"What in the world can a little kid be doing out at this time of night?" Peg asked. John shook his head, flipped off the living room light and started up the stairs — but he could not go on. He felt he must make some attempt to find out who the child was. He went to the front door and opened it to look out. It was a cold clear night and he could see plainly to the end of the street. No one was in sight.

"Maybe we ought to call the police," Peg suggested.

"Maybe," he said, and then, "Listen!"

Again they heard the plaintive cry, "Mommy, Daddy ..." coming now from the direction they first had heard it. They stood in the darkened room listening to the frightened young voice coming closer until it was in front of their house. John looked out the window again.

"Peg, look!" he said. A little boy about their son's age stood in front of the house, looking up with a mournful expression.

Again he cried, "Mommy, Daddy ..." and he turned his footsteps up the walk to the front door. John ran to open it but at the same time he felt a strange irrational fear. Peg, whose natural instinct would have been to run to bring in the child, instead had retreated into the kitchen.

When John looked out the door the child was no longer in sight. He looked up and down the street but there was nothing to see, not even footprints on the light snow. They no longer heard the voice. He stepped back into the house, feeling a chill that was caused by more than the frigid air.

With an almost unbearable shock, again they heard the voice, "Mommy, Daddy ...." Peg caught John's arm. This time the voice came from inside the house, from upstairs. Together they rushed up to Johnny's room. He cried, "Mommy, Daddy, I was lost and I couldn't find my way home. I was so cold!"

— *Carl R. Perrin, Defiance, Ohio*
December 1968

Interrupted Journey

I was scheduled for surgery on March 15, 1969, at New York City's Columbia Presbyterian Hospital. On the operating table I was told to relax and to breathe deeply through the mask over my face. I sank into oblivion and knew nothing more until a terrible constriction seized my chest. I struggled desperately to breathe but I could not. For an endless time the agony was unbearable. I remember vividly the utter panic I felt as I thought, "I'm dying. I've got to get out of here!"

And suddenly I was out, speeding into vast dark space. I seemed no larger than a dot and I was moving at an incredible rate when suddenly I was pulled up short. I found myself suspended between two other dots!

I seemed to be held there while we communicated without words. A feeling of great joy came over me, a sense of pure love and total bliss like nothing I've ever experienced. But "they" told me I could not stay, that I had made a mistake and must go back.

Without volition I was propelled back at the same tremendous speed toward a voice calling me from a great distance. Now panic-stricken, I seemed to scream: "Wait for me. I am coming and I cannot answer you through my body until I get there!"

Next I felt a burning sensation at the site of the operation and I realized the incision was being cleaned with alcohol. I responded to the nurse who was calling my name. I came to on the operating table; it was all over.

My doctor, Myron C. Roberts, told me afterwards that there had been some trouble, but it was nothing to concern myself about. I could have told him that and more!

— *Lee Dal Cero, Lindenhurst, New York*
July 1970

To Die ... Is to Live!

The 28-year-old woman from Ord, Nebraska, suffered from a defective mitral valve believed to have stemmed from rheumatic fever in 1942. With time, her failing heart grew so tremendous as to fill both sides of the chest. Doctors scheduled her for surgery to correct the valve.

I was that patient.

At the Mayo Clinic on March 7, 1958, a surgical staff of 18, headed by Dr. Kirkland and Dr. Henry Ellis, Jr., operated at St. Mary's Hospital, a part of the Mayo Clinic. The surgery lasted from 7:30 A.M. to 1:30 P.M.

It must have been in the recovery room, still deeply anaesthetized, that I became aware that my mental activity had heightened to an extraordinary degree. I saw myself clearly as a little girl, a young lady and a woman. In a powerful, intense, living dream I witnessed a panoramic view of my life. At the same time I could hear delightful music.

As my consciousness grew more acute, my vision also extended. I could see what was going on behind my back, in the next room, even in distant places. Incongruously, I wondered if I should close my eyes. I tried to, but found I couldn't! I no longer had control of my body. I thought, "I'm dead!" Yet how could I think, hear and see more clearly than ever before?

From somewhere outside my body came great engulfing waves of emotion, the sadness of my parents, Mr. and Mrs. Joseph Mantia, who had come from Washington, D.C., to be with me. My increased sensitivity made me feel and understand their grief with an intensity formerly unknown to me.

My life continued to unroll before me and now I saw the purpose of it. All bitterness was wiped out. I knew the meaning of every event and I saw its place in a great pattern. Although much that was crystal clear that morning has become veiled again since then, I never have forgotten the sense of eternal order and rightness that came to me that day.

For the first time, I looked with astonishment and joy at the real me, the real self, while a sepulcher of clay enclosed the old me. I beheld the wonders of my body and knew it was intimately interwoven, tissue for tissue, with the living soul of that dead physical form.

Realizing my condition, I reasoned calmly that I had died, as humans understand death, and I was about to get out of my physical body. I sensed and heard, it seemed, the snapping of innumerable small cords — and then I was free.

I remember clearly how I appeared to myself, formless and colorless. I floated up like a soap bubble, then fell lightly to the floor where I rose and expanded to my full height. I seemed to be translucent and I knew I was naked. Feeling a painful embarrassment, I fled toward the partly opened door to escape the eyes of two nurses and others I knew were around me, but when I reached the door I found myself clothed!

I turned back and, as I turned, my left elbow brushed the arm of one of the doctors. To my surprise his arm passed through mine. I looked quickly at his face to see if he had noticed the contact but he gave no sign. He stood gazing toward the bed I had just left.

When I looked back at my intact physical form, it occurred to me to wonder how I could see not only obvious things but through the doctor. I could even see the straight seam down the back of the nightgown on the figure on the bed. I felt for my eyes. They were where they should be. Then I discovered an infinitesimal cord, no thicker than a spider's web, running from my shoulders back to my body and attached to it at the base of the neck. I concluded that through that cord I could use the eyes. Turning, I started down the hall.

Suddenly a small dense black cloud appeared in front of me and advanced toward my face. I knew I was to be stopped. I felt the power to move and to think leaving me. My hands fell powerless at my sides. My shoulders, neck and head dropped forward and I knew no more.

With no effort on my part my eyes opened. I looked at my flesh-and-blood hands and then at the bed in wonderment. Realizing I was back in my body I said in astonishment and disappointment, "What in the world has happened to me? Must I die again?"

I realize I must, but dying is no longer a terrifying experience. I speak as one who started on the path and then came back. It taught me to live.

— *Constance M. Kluna, Fergus Falls, Minnesota*
June 1970

I Met the Great Spirit

Our small boat capsized on a cold trout lake in mid-February 1990, near Forsyth, Missouri. My companion drowned, but I survived because I was wearing a life jacket.

It took me nearly an hour to reach shore. It was dark by then. With no source of warmth, I removed my clothes, wrung them out, then put them back on, still damp. I stuffed dry leaves under my clothes for insulation. It was very cold — 10 degrees Fahrenheit — and ice formed on my wet clothes. I sat against a large tree, shivering so violently it hurt. My background is Cherokee Indian, and I prayed to the Great Spirit for help.

I realized I might not survive the night. I recalled how American Indians in battle often said, "It's a good day to die." I thought about them as the cold surrounded me like a fierce animal.

Surprisingly, my mind was peaceful. I judged I'd been in the cold for about five hours. Suddenly, I found my conscious mind slightly above the trees. I was viewing my body on the ground. There was no Jesus there, no angel, no white light. But I did feel that I was enfolded, body and soul, in care and love — indescribable love, accompanied by soft flute music. I felt nothing but joy. I don't know how long I was in this state, but suddenly I was back in my body, cold and lonely again. Then again I was above the trees, embraced in love and music. I passed from the treetops back to my body several times, until a beautiful force urged me back into my body for good.

When morning came I started out for help. For more than eight hours I crawled and walked over rough Ozark mountain terrain. I finally found a house — just three miles away.

At the hospital, the nurse said my core temperature was 88 degrees, and my fingers and feet were frostbitten. It took about six hours to bring my temperature up to the normal 98.6.

I know now that I was blessed by the Great Spirit, and I have no fear of death. I am healthy and happy.

— *Freddie Booker, Forsyth, Missouri*
June 1997

If This Be Death

I learned about death in 1923. During lunch on August 14 of that year I fainted in our home in Brinkley, Arkansas. My husband, Ted Clemons, rushed me to the hospital where doctors found that my appendix was ruptured and gangrenous. I was immediately prepared for surgery.

As the ether cone brought oblivion, I discovered I could see through walls! I was high above the people around me and seemed to see everything at once.

I saw the nurses and visitors moving through the hall and heard two student nurses whispering about the terminal surgery in progress. The small hospital had only one operating room so the terminal case had to be me. How silly! I felt fine.

Suddenly I remembered my mother. I approached the nurse who had prepared me for surgery and touched her arm saying, "Nurse, please ask my husband if he has called our families."

She didn't seem to have heard me but she shuddered slightly and said to an aide, "Ask Mr. Clemons if there is anyone he'd like us to call. He's so upset he probably hasn't thought of it."

The aide went to Ted, whose face was very white. He left briefly to call.

After several hours, the door marked "Surgery" opened and a sheeted cart emerged guided by the anaesthetist, a nurse, and my surgeon, Dr. Blanton. Ted held open the door to my room and, as they passed in, I went along. I stood in a corner watching as they carefully placed my inert body in bed, tucking the covers close but leaving an opening for the stethoscope, which Dr. Blanton quickly applied. He listened a few seconds, then turned to Ted.

"Mr. Clemons, we have done our best but it may not be enough. She'll be unconscious for several hours. Sit with her if you like but don't try to talk to her. She can't hear you."

Unconscious indeed! The doctor left and the nurse took up her station beside my bed constantly checking my pulse. Bored by the talk of my imminent demise, I moved into the hall. Never had I felt more alert and alive.

Several hours later my mother, Rhoda Russell, and my sister, Ellen Turner, arrived from Poplar Bluff, Missouri. When I saw how worried they looked I wondered if I might be buried alive. That was not an idle thought; in those days only the rich were embalmed. As these thoughts went through my mind, the room started to fade and I found myself outside, moving very fast.

I rose above the buildings in a wide spiral. The sun was more colorful than I'd ever imagined. The trees were green and everything seemed to have a bright glistening look. I gained momentum until I actually soared, and then I felt suddenly that I should go back. I didn't hear a voice of command or any sound, but I knew I had to return.

I had no wish to return to the bondage of my body and bed, but a strong tug at the nape of my neck pulled me backward very fast.

Then I was flowing — that's the only word for the feeling — though reluctantly, into my inert body, and feeling each part and organ activating as I did so. The narrow confining area of my body was uncomfortable. I was not at all happy about it.

When she saw my eyes move the astonished nurse ran for the doctor. I was dismissed from the hospital on September 3, 1923.

I shall never forget that wonderful experience. If death is like that, what is there to fear?

— *Grace R. Jaco, Cape Girardeau, Missouri*
July 1970

Was I a Ghost?

I was ill in the hospital in Mora, in eastern Minnesota, eight years ago. My roommate, Mrs. Markhart, of Giese, Minnesota, a dear old lady of 88, was also very ill. Neither of us was expected to recover, and when I overheard a doctor ask the nurse on duty if it was all right to call Reverend Olson for Mrs. Molin, I realized how limited my time was thought to be. I was resigned to whatever would be, but Mrs. Markhart continually hoped and prayed that she might see her daughter, Mrs. Ann Helen Lennert, who lived in Miles City, Montana, once more upon this earth. I prayerfully hoped with her. More, I thought, I could not do.

How or when I left the hospital, I cannot remember. Perhaps I did not make the trip physically but I feel that I did. However, I could not have been gone more than 24 hours or another patient would have occupied my bed and of course this is not long enough for the trip I remember. On the other hand, Mrs. Hunt, the registered nurse on duty at Kanabec Hospital at that time, spoke to me of my absence. Her tour of duty was eight hours and I must have been away from my bed for some of that time. It is strange that some things concerning the trip are so vivid in my mind and others are disconnected, vague and seemingly impossible. I do not attempt to explain it, only to tell you what happened.

I remember recognizing the names of the towns as I rode by train through North Dakota, for I had lived in that state at one time. It was February 1950, winter and cold. I was glad to stop to warm myself at the railway station when I got off the train at Miles City, my destination.

Then I walked to a beautiful old home. I do not know the street address because I am not well acquainted with Miles City, having spent only one summer there before this unexpected visit. I walked into the house as I would at home. I felt I belonged there although I had never entered the place before. I passed through two rooms into a bedroom occupied by a sick woman. She was not startled, for besides looking very much like me, she felt the same deep sense of kinship I felt at that moment. This woman was Ann Helen Lennert, my hospital roommate's yearned-for daughter. I had come to take her back with me and asked her to be ready soon.

I waited in another room until she joined me, well dressed and looking fine. She left a note for her husband and we departed by bus. While stopping at the bus depot at Grand Forks, North Dakota, I remember signing a blue traveler's card and this act must have been responsible for the beautiful travel literature which I began to receive about three weeks later.

I was comfortable in bed again in the hospital when the nurse, Mrs. Hunt, came to tuck us in for the night.

"Patients are not to leave the hospital alone," she chided. "When did you get back?"

Everything now seemed so strange to me that I could give her no answer.

The next morning my new friend, Ann Helen Lennert, stopped at my bed to thank me for bringing her to be with her mother. She said she would not have come otherwise.

That night her mother died.

What force enabled my mind or my body to go on a mission that could not have been accomplished any other way? In the limited time, in my dying condition, how could I have gone? And yet somehow I fetched a daughter to her dying mother's bedside in time.

— *Anne Molin, Ogilvie, Minnesota*
January 1961

A Red Balloon

I was only 13 when, on April 1, 1964, an accidental fire left me with second- and third-degree burns. I was rushed to the hospital, but due to the severity of the burns my veins collapsed. As if in a hellish nightmare, doctors told my mother, Alice Graves, that I had only 15, then 10, then five minutes to live.

Mom, numb with anguish, could only watch and pray. Doctors, standing shoulder to shoulder around my bed, worked feverishly. Seconds later a Japanese doctor found a vein, saving my life.

During this time I was in a coma, unaware that my life was in danger. While comatose I saw a friend whom I knew as Belinda Michelle, who had previously died. She asked me to go with her. She had a red balloon that we played with as we left.

I was thrust into a period of darkness. The darkness was like a swift slide through a warm tunnel. At the tunnel's end was an indescribably beautiful pasture and stream.

Suddenly we were on a ski lift. I was very confused. My friend, sensing this, assured me I would understand. Soon we passed signs reading 15 miles, 10 miles, five miles. The miles on the signs correlated with the doctor's prognoses.

Upon passing the third sign, my friend told me I could go no further. I awoke to excruciating pain. My mom, rushing to my side, handed me a red balloon.

— *Holly Kimber Graves, St. Petersburg, Florida*
January 1991

REINCARNATION

I was drawn to this house and thought I had lived in it before, though my mother denied it (and she wouldn't lie to me). Yet I knew its rooms and furniture, even the window drapes.
— *From Jean Brown's "I've Been Here Before," page 179*

Central to the ancient teachings of Hinduism, Buddhism, Theosophy, and Spiritualism, reincarnation gives us a chance to right Karmic wrongs in the next life. Researchers including Allan Kardec, Sir Arthur Conan Doyle, and Professor Hans Holzer (author of *Born Again: The Truth about Reincarnation*, Doubleday, 1970) subjected numerous cases of reported reincarnations to the light of scientific methodology. In a 1990 article for FATE Magazine, Holzer wrote, "When we are dealing with 'outsiders' to the system of reincarnation, the vast uncommitted and often hostile world of ordinary people ... [we] must present strong, direct and no-nonsense evidence that we are dealing with facts, not belief systems. ... It is that strong conviction, based on demonstrated fact, which has made it possible for me to view reincarnation in general as a natural part of human existence, common to all."

I've Been Here Before

In 1941, when I was seven, I often asked my mother, Lillian Lenore Van Arsdale, to take me to a house on Main Street, between 9th and 10th streets, in Belmar, New Jersey. I was drawn to this house and thought I had lived in it before, though my mother denied it (and she wouldn't lie to me). Yet I knew its rooms and furniture, even the window drapes.

Mother was concerned and at times angry with me as I chattered relentlessly. I even told her all about the woman living there — what she looked like, what she wore while cleaning the house, and I described her cooking apron. Although my mother said I had not been inside, I could picture it clearly: In the entrance, next to the front door, hung a long mirror with wood carvings on the top. There were gold coat racks on either side of it, and a bench nearby.

There was a long table in the dining room to the right. At the table were eight dark wooden chairs, with big, high backs and blue cloth seats. Only the two chairs at the ends of the table had arms on them. A picture of three horses' heads hung on the left wall. I will never forget it. There were big gas lights in the dining room as well, one on each side of the picture, and one on either side of the two windows on the right wall, overlooking the front porch.

I described the tablecloth — white lace covering the same blue cloth that was on the chairs. A tall, dark wood-and-glass china hutch was on the longest wall. In it were many pretty blue dishes and blue water glasses with long stems.

There were three bedrooms upstairs. The first room on the left was the biggest, containing a bed as high as my shoulders. The headboard almost reached the ceiling, and was carved with pictures of flowers, baskets and ribbons. On this bed was a white bedspread I often described to my mother, but she wouldn't believe me. She said I had never ever been inside.

When I cried for the umpteenth time, Mother took me by the hand, walked right up to the front door, and rang the bell.

A pretty woman answered the door, and I was sure I had seen her before. I knew the ring on her hand, and the apron she wore was the same as the one I had described. I stood still and held my breath. She welcomed us in.

While she and my mother talked in hushed tones, my eyes roamed around the entrance hall and into the dining room. When we went in, everything was as I had described. My mom was surprised, but the lady was shocked and had tears in her eyes. She hugged me tightly for a long time. Mom thanked her, and was glad that I was satisfied. I was happy that Mom finally believed me. My compelling urge was gone.

One day I heard Mom telling my aunt, Emma Gifford, that a little five-year-old girl who had lived in that house died of scarlet fever on May 23, 1934, the year I was born. After that we never talked about it again. Mother said I "should not ask to go there again."

I never did. I then believed that I knew the little girl very well, but as I grew older, I realized this was not so. I remember more things about her and the house when I see blue glasses or white lace table cloths. Could I really have been her, keeping some of her memories?

— *Jean Brown, New Underwood, South Dakota*
February 1994

Did Donald Drown Twice?

I generally believe that phobias are acquired but my younger son Donald was born with his: an acute fear of water. I gave him his first bath when he was four days old, newly arrived from Ingalls Memorial Hospital in Harvey, Illinois, where he had been born August 29, 1960, and he screamed in terror.

After that, bathing Donald and washing his hair were tasks I dreaded, knowing they would be accompanied by stentorian shrieks. What a contrast to his older brother Paul; he loved water. For him I filled the bathtub almost to the rim and put heavy rubber toys on the bottom. He dived in to retrieve the toys, laughing gleefully when he surfaced with all of them in his hands. When Donald was old enough to use the regular bathtub, he would tolerate only about two inches of water and still he screamed and clung to my arm until his bath was over. Surely, I thought, Donald will outgrow this inordinate fear of water. When he's older he will want to swim with other children.

My husband Paul was the Cub master when our sons joined the Boy Scouts and one of the merit badges to be earned was for swimming. We were living in Park Forest, Illinois, and Paul arranged with the local YMCA for the Cub Scouts' use of the pool. On the first day of class one of the two instructors told the boys to line up on the diving board at the deep end of the pool and jump into the water one by one; the other instructor would catch them. The boys were assured they were in no danger even though they couldn't swim. Each of the eight- and nine-year-olds jumped fearlessly into the water, hugely enjoying the trip to the shallow end in the arms of the instructor.

Donald was last in line. Reluctantly he walked the length of the diving board and stopped.

"Come on, Donald, jump!" said the instructor in the water. "I'll catch you."

"I'm afraid," Donald mumbled. All of his friends were trying to encourage him but he stood stock-still. Perhaps not understanding that this was more than ordinary fear, the instructor on the diving board gave Donald a push. His action was not expeditious enough, however, and Donald grabbed his leg and pulled him into the water too.

While the other boys learned to swim in the shallow end of the pool, Donald clung to the side. Soon all of the boys were swimming confidently in deep water and Donald couldn't swim a stroke. The others earned their merit badges but his father couldn't give one to Donald.

Earlier, when Donald was about six, he became fascinated with the *Titanic* disaster. My brother-in-law Joe Voss gave him a thick book on the subject — more than 1,000 pages — and Donald had read it from cover to cover by the time he was seven. He became a self-taught expert on the *Titanic*. He could tell you who designed and built it, the names of every passenger and crew member on board, the number of lifeboats, the ships that ignored distress signals and of course the hymn that was sung and played as the ship sank. He seemed to know every nut and bolt that went into the building of the gargantuan vessel.

I was a little disturbed when he began to grieve for the people who had lost their lives in the disaster. He raged that there weren't enough lifeboats to save everyone.

"No one should have drowned," he said angrily. "They should have had 48 lifeboats to save everyone. It was the White Star Line's fault that they didn't have enough."

"Did the book say that?" I asked.

"No," he replied, "but I said that 16 lifeboats weren't enough."

"Well, they thought that the ship was unsinkable," I replied. "But you're right. They should have had enough lifeboats to save everyone."

"The ship wasn't unsinkable," Donald argued. "There were lots of places where water could get in. The White Star Line knew that."

One day Donald said musingly, "Two children used to play in an empty room on the *Titanic*. They played there all day long."

"Does your book even say that?" I asked.

"No, but they liked it better than on the deck."

At the time these remarks didn't seem to have any significance but I often thought it was unusual for a seven-year-old boy to be so fascinated by a disaster that occurred so long ago.

He often talked about the screams of the doomed passengers and the icy cold water of the North Atlantic. "It was so cold," he said. "When you swallowed it, it was icy and salty and made you choke. It was freezing out there and there was nothing to hold on to. The band kept playing until the ship went down. They should have had more lifeboats!"

The years went by and still Donald hadn't learned to swim. As a teenager he took showers with the bathroom door open and asked that I stay in the house until he finished. Eventually this irrational phobia embarrassed him and he pleaded with me not to tell anyone.

Then one summer our neighbor George Walker had a regulation below-ground swimming pool installed in his backyard and he invited our family to use it. Donald could see that all of us were having a marvelous time, swimming, diving and playing water games, and he decided at last that he was ready to learn to swim. I taught him basic strokes in the shallow end and he was surprised and pleased to discover that he didn't sink like a stone. He gained confidence and even dived for rings, coins, and stones in the deepest part of the pool. He learned to be a fairly good, although by no means expert, swimmer.

On July 12, 1980, while on a camping trip with friends, Donald drowned in a quarry near Braidwood, Illinois. Although only 20 feet from shore, when he discovered it was 30 feet to the bottom, he panicked. Two helpless non-swimming companions on shore who heard him scream for help couldn't save our 19-year-old son.

At his memorial service we asked the organist to play the hymn "Nearer My God to Thee." The hymn the band played as the *Titanic* sank seemed appropriate for Donald.

Some months later I saw a television documentary on the *Titanic* disaster which featured interviews with survivors.

One elderly woman said, "My brother and I were children then. We used to play all day in an empty room ...."

Donald had said, "Two children used to play in an empty room ... all day long."

Architectural drawings of the Titanic did indeed show vulnerable areas where water could enter if a hole were gouged in the ship's skin.

Donald had said, "There were lots of places water could get in. The White Star Line knew that."

One of the crewmen on the documentary said that there had been only 16 lifeboats and there should have been at least 48. "Sixty-four would have been even better," he said.

Donald had said, "They should have had 48 lifeboats to save everyone. I said that 16 lifeboats weren't enough."

Other persons on the documentary spoke of screams coming from the frigid water; when Donald talked of the cold, salty, choking water, it was as if he knew firsthand.

Is it possible that Donald drowned twice?

— *Sue Heron Wollam*
July 1983

My Other Mommy and Daddy

One day in January 1983, I was fixing lunch for my oldest daughter, Cassie, who was three years old. As I put the finishing touches on the tuna fish salad, she came over to me and insisted I hold her hand. "Honey, Mommy can't finish lunch with only one hand," I said, but she continued to hold my right hand.

She looked up at me seriously and said, "Mommy, we are very lucky to have food today."

I was a little shocked, since she had never been without.

She said, "Mommy, why did my other mommy and daddy not have enough food?"

"Honey, what other mommy and daddy?" I asked.

"You know, the mommy and daddy I lived with before I lived with you. How come we can live in a nice warm house and my other mommy and daddy can't?" she asked.

I didn't know what to say. Was she thinking of her grandparents? Her grandparents — James and Margie Bell, and Frank and Clythel Rees — had nice homes and plenty of food on the table. I stopped what I was doing and sat down with Cassie. "Tell Mommy about your other mommy and daddy," I prompted her.

She answered my questions, describing the house and conditions where she said she had lived, which were by the train tracks. She was always cold and hungry, and the last thing she remembered was being very ill. To this day, Cassie worries if the refrigerator starts to look a little bare. I believe she was remembering a past life, one that still affects her life today, even though she does not remember telling me about it.

After Cassie told me about her other parents, I read several books on the subject and found that this was a common occurrence. Sadly, that's as far as I could take my research, since she was unable to give me names, dates, or locations. Hypnotherapists have also been suggested, but that should be Cassie's decision when she's old enough.

— *Dora Rees, Sahuarita, Arizona*
December 1993

The Century-Old Nightmare

I had a series of nightmares in 1945 when I was five years old. In those dreams I was a child lying in bed in a house totally unlike ours. It was made of logs and the floors were rough-hewn pine boards. A candle burned brightly on a wooden table. Everything seemed peaceful — at first.

Then I would hear a woman's scream and a commotion at the other end of the house — angry shouts, a rifle shot, more screams. I was sitting up in bed, every nerve in my body quivering with fear. Several men dressed in blue uniforms rushed past my room.

Then I heard a woman cry out, "No, don't kill him. Please!" One of the men struck her and another rushed toward me. His eyes were burning with hatred and he carried a large knife on a long stick. He was about to stab me!

At that point in the dream I would always wake up screaming. The dream came every night, always the same, for about two weeks — and then stopped. I had almost forgotten those nightmares until 34 years later, when I went to see a psychic who gave past-life readings.

With the tape recorder going, she immediately saw me as a five-year-old boy in a log cabin in Virginia in the 1860s. Some renegade Union soldiers were rushing toward my home. They broke down the door, demanding food and money. My mother screamed and pleaded with them not to harm me. She was killed and one of the men charged toward me with his bayonet. I tried to get up and he plunged the bayonet into my chest.

Although the psychic knew absolutely nothing about my childhood nightmares, she explained them by telling me about a past existence. And when I learned that it sometimes took a couple of weeks for the bodies of civilian victims of the Civil War to be discovered, I felt I had solved yet another mystery: My nightmares lasted two weeks. Perhaps it took that long for my body to be discovered and finally laid to rest.

— Tom Mach, Sidney, Ohio
November 1983

Crippled by a Past Life

In the early 1950s I was hopelessly crippled by arthritis. Leading physicians in Houston, Fort Worth, and Dallas, Texas, all had examined me and arrived at the same conclusion.

"There is nothing more that we can do," I was told. "We know that the pain in your back is excruciating but we can promise no cure. You will be able to walk as long as you wear a steel brace and we can give you relief from the severe pain. You must adjust your life to this."

After Dr. Marvin Knight, an eminent bone specialist from Dallas, fitted me with the steel brace I began the forlorn task of accepting this limited and painful existence. For a person as active as I had been the adjustment was difficult to make. Moreover, my clothes had to be altered to accommodate the brace, which made me feel and look ponderous. This condition injured my ego almost as much as the disease hurt my back.

But I still had my mind. Along with my sister Margaret, who had stuck with me through all these agonizing experiences, I pursued my interest in psychology, taking courses at three universities and studying not only the orthodox works on psychology but also the claims of far-out cults and societies.

When L. Ron Hubbard's bestselling *Dianetics:The Modern Science of Mental Health* appeared, we read it avidly. Shortly afterwards we attended a lecture on the subject given by Ross Lamareaux in Dallas. We went in a skeptical mood, for we thought that the techniques Mr. Hubbard outlined in his book were much too simple to effectively straighten out quirks in the mind.

The lecture, held in a private home, attracted about 30 people who sat crowded together in the living room. Mr. Lamareaux gave a short talk on dianetics in which he explained that the treatment was carried out by what he called auditors. He said that he was going to give us a demonstration of how auditing works, then asked for a volunteer for the session. Without thinking I raised my hand immediately.

As Mr. Lamareaux seated me in front of him in a straight-backed chair, he noticed there was something wrong with my back from the awkward manner in which I sat and asked me what the trouble was. I explained.

Then, as if out of nowhere, he asked, "If you wanted to hurt someone, how would you do it?"

"I'd hit him in the back with a big stick," I replied. As soon as I'd said it, I was puzzled. I could not recall ever striking anyone in the back with a big stick.

Mr. Lamareaux leaned near me and said, "Can you imagine that you have a big stick in your hands?" I nodded. "Now feel that stick," he said. "Feel its roughness, its thickness. Now hit down with that stick. Hit hard."

I remember feeling how silly that was, how silly I must look to the other guests. But Ross paid no attention to the others. His large brown eyes staring deep into mine, he disregarded the skeptical smile on my face.

"Hit harder," he went on. "Hit as though you really wanted to hurt someone."

I thought, "If this is Mr. Hubbard's idea of psychology it's pretty damn silly." But since I had volunteered I was determined to go along with whatever he had in mind. With a shrug of my shoulders and a smug smile I hit down. "Again," Ross said. "Again." This time I hit with such force that I felt a pain in my back.

Suddenly the whole scene changed. I was in another world. No longer conscious of Ross or of anything in that room I became a different person, not the awkward woman in a brace, sitting in a chair in this modern home. Margaret said later that she could tell the moment I changed. The confident smile disappeared from my face and a look of wonderment — a strange look in my eyes — replaced it.

I still can see the scene that stretched before me. I was standing in the backyard of a peculiar-looking house with a large girl, fair of complexion, with long blond hair. I don't know how but I knew that the girl was myself. There was no doubt. I also knew that I was 12 years old.

At the back of a low house was an overhanging thatched roof; the house was composed of small rough stones held together by a sort of mud. A large flat stone that served as a step lay in front of a small wooden door. About 10 yards from the house there was another much larger flat stone, this one irregular in shape but completely flat and about two feet thick. Two hundred feet away I could see a long low fence also made of small rocks.

I was not alone in that barren rocky yard. James — whom I had loved for two years, first as a child, now as nearly a woman — sat before me. He was a large brawny young man with a wealth of reddish hair worn much in the style of today's hippies. Easy of manner to the point of arrogance, he watched me, flashing a smile barely short of contemptuous.

I waited there trembling, waiting for some sign that would tell me that he took pleasure in my company. But he made no response. I called out his name and would have said more, but he turned away from me and stretched out lazily on the flat rock. Furious, I picked up a large stick, walked over to where he rested and in a flash of passion struck him on his back. He lay there stunned and speechless for a minute, then slowly turned over and rose. He still was smiling but as he entered the house I noticed with satisfaction that he clasped both hands tightly to his back. Not until he was inside did I realize that I had hurt him badly. I ran crying to the long low fence at the rear of the yard where I sobbed out, "I didn't mean it, James, I didn't mean it!"

Suddenly I heard the voice of Ross asking, "Where are you?" I resented his intrusion on my grief but I answered, "England."

"Where in England?"

"Cumberland County."

"Who are you? What is your name?" Ross had come nearer to me but I did not see him.

"Arnette," I said. "Arnette Bowen."

"What year is it?"

"1632," I snapped, as if anyone in his right mind should know what year it was.

For the next few minutes I seemed to be suspended between two worlds. I no longer was sobbing but emotionally I was torn between grief at my vicious attack on James and annoyance at Ross' continual prying into my private world.

Then I could hear Ross pulling me back. "Come up to present time," he said soothingly. "You will come up to present time."

Then my mind cleared and I could see Ross again. I remember wiping my eyes, for they were still wet with tears.

"Mrs. Elliott, you are in present time. Your back may be a little sore tomorrow so I would advise you to go to an auditor and have him or her run this for you."

Clumsily I made my way to the chair beside Margaret, who sat wide-eyed and alarmed.

When Ross attempted to continue his lecture, he discovered that he had lost his audience. Everyone wanted to know what had happened, why I had called out "James!" and sobbed, "I didn't mean it, I didn't mean it." Margaret kept pressing me, "Ada, what happened to you? Are you sure you're all right?"

Acceding to the wishes of the group Ross asked me if I would tell them exactly what I had seen.

Much later — weary from all the questions I had been asked — I left for home with Margaret. We had much to discuss. We both realized that whether or not Ross had done it intentionally there was no doubt that I had been in a deep hypnotic trance.

We sat late that night pondering the clear implication of the evening's experience; there well might be a connection between the events of that other life and the condition of my back in this one.

By the next morning — just as Ross had predicted — my back was indeed very sore. We recognized, of course, that the suggestion conceivably could have caused this. In an attempt to allay the pain I called a woman — whose name I cannot recall — for an appointment to remove the suggestion, though I did not mention hypnosis.

The woman who questioned me in her home was at a loss how to proceed. She knew the routine methods she had been taught but had had no experience with a former life episode. She was kind and did her best but she did not know how to handle that situation.

By the next morning I was in excruciating pain and Margaret and I berated ourselves for being foolish enough to let our curiosity get us into such a predicament.

"Of course you didn't have to volunteer," Margaret said. "I'm going to call that Ross Lamareaux in Fort Worth."

When she did she told him, "You got her in this condition and now you get her out of it."

Much disturbed, Ross asked if I was able to come to Fort Worth. If not he would come to Dallas. She told him that she would bring me to him and so with the help of aspirin and my brace we made the short trip to Fort Worth.

We met Ross at the home of Jack and Mary Blackman, old friends of ours.

I do not recall every question I was asked in the course of that six-hour session. Ross had me relive over and over the scene that I had witnessed as Arnette Bowen. In the beginning I would sense the pain, the anger, the remorse, and start to cry. With each succeeding time I relived the experience, the emotion began to drain off — and wonder of wonders, so did the pain. I nearly shouted my relief.

Later, as we sat around the table in the kitchen drinking coffee, Jack said, "Now, you can take off that damn brace."

Ross said little in the course of our exchange. "Of course it follows," he said once, never explaining what he meant.

In my own case I was thinking, "Will this last? This is almost too good to be true."

Mary said quietly, "I don't think you'll have any more trouble with your back, Ada. But don't try to force anything. You'll know soon enough if you can discard that brace."

For the next few days I was afraid to leave it off. Finally one day Margaret suggested that I take it off for a short period and see if I experienced any pain. I did so and discovered there was no pain. It took me two weeks to entirely discard that heavy encasement of steel. In two more weeks I took the board off my bed, bought a good firm innerspring mattress, and proceeded to sleep in comfort.

All this happened in 1951. Twenty years have passed since that memorable evening when I relived the experience of the young English girl, Arnette Bowen. And in all this time I have experienced no recurrence of the trouble in my back.

Was it karma that had carried through several generations during which I paid my debt for inflicting pain? Did hypnosis, used by wise and open-minded people, bring this memory to the surface and release the energy held in it?

— *Ada Elliott*
May 1971

I Was Horatio on the Bridge

Way back when I was only nine years old, I began to reason, even if only subconsciously, that I had led a prior existence sometime in the remote past.

Even today I can vividly recall my initial "flashback" into a former existence. It happened while I was seated in class one day while attending fourth grade in the Pine Street Elementary School in Hamden. I was daydreaming, looking out the window, when I felt compelled to sketch an elaborate drawing.

I took a large sheet of plain white paper and began to fill in a scene that was going through my mind. The completed drawing showed a narrow stone bridge upon which a lone soldier, a sentry, dressed in the battle gear of a Roman warrior, stood at one end of the bridge seemingly protecting it from an enemy horde approaching from the other side. This figure, carrying various spears and a colorful shield, was holding back the massed opposing army single-handedly.

I remember looking at the completed sketch for a long time and thinking the scene seemed familiar. But at the time I had not as yet read Macauley's poem, "Horatio at the Bridge." Not until several years later in high school, in fact, did we study the famous poem about the legendary Horatius Cocles. The Roman hero defended his homeland by protecting the bridge across the Tiber River during an attempted invasion by the Etruscan Army until other soldiers could be brought in to lend him support. His courageous action saved the city and Horatio's valiant efforts were immortalized.

As a fourth-grader, looking at the sketch I had made, I seemed to be drawn into it, almost as if I had some strange connection with this historic era and with Horatio in particular. It was uncanny.

It was not until years later, when I had grown to manhood, that what had actually transpired grew clearer. I was talking to a woman one day who was reputed to have great psychic powers. For no reason at all she stared at me and said, "Ernest, I see an orange-red glow around you." Pausing momentarily, as if looking right through me into some void beyond, she said, "I see you in the uniform of a Roman soldier. In fact — yes, you were Horatio at the bridge."

To say the least, I was jolted — and yet I knew she was absolutely correct. I had been battling inwardly against accepting what should have been crystal clear to me all this time.

— *Ernest Borgnine*
February 1975

ALIEN ENCOUNTERS

"Nobody knows it, Walter, but I am not from this world."
— *From Walter H. Arden's "They Are Among Us," page 195*

While skepticism concerning alien encounters runs high, Roper Poll findings suggest that two percent of the U.S. population, or about five million people, have had experiences consistent with a UFO abduction. And who are the abductors? Greys are the usual suspects, but other oft-cited alien races include Nordics, large praying mantises, reptilians, and giants. Theories about their origins, actions, and intentions abound, and as the following firsthand reports show, getting a definitive answer may prove to be a daunting task.

They Are Among Us

I was the lodge master of a German/American Freemason lodge in San Francisco, California. On a cold Monday night in December 1966, I had just closed the weekly meeting, and, as was my habit, I was waiting until the last lodge member had left so I could turn off the lights.

One lodge brother was still present, putting on his overcoat and hat. His name was Richard Decker. He was a slight, white-haired gentleman in his seventies who owned an engineering business in San Francisco.

I had always had a special liking for Richard. He seemed to have few, if any, friends among his lodge brothers, perhaps because he always displayed a very reserved manner. He did not partake in the lodge's social events, and I never saw him laugh or even smile. When Richard spoke, it was short, precisely to the point, and without embellishment. He had earned the reputation for only saying what was absolutely correct, reliable, and truthful, and it was this character trait that had earned him my friendship and esteem.

When Richard approached me that night to shake hands and say good-bye, I noticed that he wore a silvery metal ornament on the lapel of his overcoat. It was shaped like a small, round flower head and had a strange, iridescent reflection that I had never seen before. I inspected the pin closely, touching it with my fingertips, and I asked Richard what its meaning was.

He said, "Walter, that is the reason for my leaving the lodge room last, because I don't want others to see it and ask me about it. I like you and I trust you, so I will answer your question, but you must give me your word that you will divulge to no one what I am going to tell you."

I agreed.

"You see, this is how we recognize each other," he said, pointing at the lapel pin.

"Richard, who recognizes whom?" I asked.

Then Richard told me this story: "Nobody knows it, Walter, but I am not from this world. I come from the star (he then mentioned a name that I had never heard of, did not understand, and therefore cannot remember). You should know that I am not alone — there are thousands of us here on Earth, and that is why we need to recognize each other."

I said, "But Richard, I know for a fact that you were born in Germany, that you came to the United States to study engineering, and that you have been a member of this lodge for a long time."

"That is all true, of course," he replied. "When one of us is assigned to a secret mission on Earth, we have the power to walk in, which means that we take over the embryo of a pregnant Earth woman, usually from a well-situated family, and we are born like any other human child. We go to school and study a profession. We may even get married and have a family. But as soon as we have reached adulthood, we begin working on our assigned mission, the nature of which is totally secret to everyone, and I cannot tell you about this either.

"When we have reached human old age, we are called back to our home star. The present one is my fourth Earth mission. Very soon I will be called back again, but I know this is not my last mission on Earth. The next mission might be after your lifetime."

Richard reminded me to keep everything I had just heard secret, shook my hand, and left the lodge room. I had to sit down for a few moments, stunned by what had been entrusted to me. Because I had known of Richard Decker's sincerity for years, I had not the slightest doubt that what he had divulged to me was the truth. I am a doctor of metaphysical science, and I firmly believe in the supernatural and the existence of extraterrestrials.

Fifteen months later, in February 1968, Richard Decker disappeared without a trace, but I knew where he was. I kept his secret for 28 years before I told my family and lodge members about it. After that length of time, I believed Richard would have considered my promise fulfilled.

— Walter H. Arden, San Raphael, California
August 1996

Audrey of Venus

In 1955, when I was 17, my sister Pattie and I had a close encounter with a huge flying saucer. Little did I know then what that experience would lead to in the following years of my life. The saucer was at least 35 feet in diameter, and it flew just over the tree tops near a shopping center in Tracy, California. It hovered over us for three to five minutes. Even though the shopping center was full of people, only my sister and I saw the craft.

Since then, I have seen many UFOs. Tracy was clearly an air corridor for both airplanes and UFOs. On two occasions, as I gazed at the night skies, I observed enormous, silent V-formations of saucers flying over the city.

In June 1957, I joined the Women's Army Corps. I was stationed in Fort McClellan, Alabama. On the first day, I noticed a girl who reminded me of myself, a kindred soul who also seemed to be a loner. We both appeared out of place. As I prepared my space in the barracks, I felt a presence, and I turned to see her standing behind me. "You believe in flying saucers, don't you?" she asked.

I was amazed. "How do you know that?" I responded.

Smiling, she said, "I know many things."

Her name was Audrey, and she was from Washington state. Her father was a UFO researcher, she said. She was quite tall and beautiful, with blonde hair, blue eyes, and fine features.

From that first day we became the best of friends. During every spare moment, she tutored me in metaphysics. I couldn't get enough. She taught about life on other worlds, galaxies, and dimensions. She was telepathic, and she taught me to astral project, and about reincarnation. She also told me that members of a certain race on Venus all had six fingers — otherwise, they closely resembled Earthlings.

During the course of our discussions, Audrey shared a strange story with me. She said she was not from Earth, but that she and her family had come here from Venus in a cigar-shaped space ship. She said they had come to help the world become more spiritual.

One day, as we sat in the company recreational room, I noticed that her hands were long and beautiful. Then I noticed that her palms extended from her little finger about two-thirds of an inch. "Why do your hands have those lumps?" I asked.

"Because I was born with six fingers and toes," she said, "and my parents had them removed so I would look normal."

Audrey's influence led me to earn a Ph.D. in Eastern metaphysics and to become an ordained minister. I have been drawn to those who have been abducted by UFOs, and I have helped them break the cycle of abductions and nightmares permanently. I am forever grateful to Audrey for pointing me in the right direction, and I am certain that we will meet again.

— *Wendy Darden Lockwood, Sonora, California*
April 1997

The Abducted Roommate

I have always been fascinated by abduction phenomena and ufology in general, but a truly strange experience woke me up to a presence that I no longer question.

About three years ago I was living in San Francisco with a roommate named Michael, who claimed that he had been abducted throughout his life. He said that beings had followed him from city to city, and that no matter where he lived, they continued to appear — usually at night. They came in the form of a bright light at first, then materialized in his bedroom. He told me that he had been abducted from the house we shared, but that he didn't tell me about his visitors, fearing that I might think he was crazy.

Three weeks later, a friend spent the night at our house. Michael went to bed about two hours before my friend and I fell asleep.

Suddenly I was completely awake! Incredibly bright lights shone through the dark curtains in all three of my bay windows. I sat straight up in bed and yelled, "The lights, the lights, do you see the lights?" My friend, fast asleep next to me, awoke and said, "What?"

She hadn't seen them, but she said that I was as white as a ghost. I told her that I awoke straight out of a sound sleep, almost as if I knew something was coming, and then the whole window lit up. I looked at the clock, which read 2:03 A.M. Despite my friend's reassurance that all was well, I couldn't fall asleep for quite some time.

The next morning I got up quietly, letting my friend sleep in, and I went to the kitchen for a bowl of cereal. Michael was fixing himself some coffee. He looked at me with a serious expression, and said, "It happened last night. I know you think my abduction stories are all made up, but they came to me around 2:00 A.M."

I almost dropped my bowl, and I told him what I had seen. Michael was relieved that I finally believed him.

I have since learned that people who are near abductees can sometimes witness such occurrences.

My views certainly changed. More than ever, I believe that I was a witness to higher intelligence, and I can more realistically and sympathetically relate to the claims of others.

> — *Lise Milner, Los Angeles*
> *January 1997*

Look! Up in the Sky!

One evening in August 1976, while driving with my husband and daughter, we spotted a friend coming out of a store in Burlington, Massachusetts. We pulled into the parking lot and got out of the car to talk to her.

My daughter, Dawna, who was six at the time, stayed in the car. As my husband, my friend, and I were talking, Dawna, watching out the car window, said, "Look, it's a flying saucer." We ignored her, as adults sometimes do when they're in conversation. She, as children sometimes do when they're ignored, repeated herself, over and over.

After the third or fourth "Look, it's a flying saucer," my husband said, "It's not a flying saucer." Then he turned to look where she was pointing, and, as he did, he said, "It's a ... FLYING SAUCER!"

Suspended in the sky above us was a huge, disk-shaped object, shimmering with white lights.

We were transfixed. Minutes seemed like hours, and we couldn't take our eyes off it.

Burlington is next to Bedford, where there was an air force base. As we stood there, looking up, we heard the sound of an airplane coming from the drection of the base. At that instant, the saucer zoomed away to the north. It was out of sight in the blink of an eye.

We jumped into our car and took off in the direction it had gone, hoping to catch sight of it again. We were unsuccessful, but we did see some young men standing by a car. We asked them if they'd seen anything. They were just as excited as we were and quite relieved, as well. It seems they'd been drinking and they thought they'd had too much.

We went home and called the air force base to ask them what we'd seen. They said it was nothing — just a plane towing something. I didn't believe them. Then, in August 1995, I saw a video on television's *Sightings* that was taken in Salida, Colorado. It reminded me of the saucer we'd seen many years before. It did not seem to be as close as the flying saucer we saw, but it did seem to be the same shape and it had the same shimmering white lights. I know now that I really did see something more than "just a plane towing something."

— *Norma Jean Hissong, Olympia, Washington*
March 1997

Encounter at Memphis Lake

In 1986, when I was 49, I suddenly felt I had lived two lives. One was normal — but it had been shaped by a string of long-repressed encounters with mysterious UFOs.

Sometime during the late 1940s or early 1950s, my family was camping with another family at Memphis State Lake near Ashland, Nebraska. Both my father and his friend Glen were wildlife conservation officers, and Glen's son Bob and I were close friends.

While we were fishing, Bob and I spotted an odd, disk-shaped craft. It hovered close to us, moving in and out of a strange blue haze. We ran to tell our parents.

Bob and his family went off in pursuit of the craft, while my mother decided it might be dangerous and told us to stay at the campground.

As we stood around, not knowing what to expect, we saw large objects directly above us. They moved in large sheets of what seemed to be flowing electric atmosphere, then disappeared behind a hill and trees.

We got into our car and followed them. Soon we met up with a large saucer sitting on the ground on the other side of the lake. It seemed as solid as our car, and it was lighted by an unseen overhead source. I remember receiving an audible communication as we sat in our car, not more than 70 feet from the craft. My whole family heard the message, and although I don't completely recall what was said, it was clear that someone wanted me inside the ship. My mother finally insisted that we leave the area.

When we encountered another craft back on the other side of the lake, I felt strongly as if someone I couldn't see was talking to me. The message told me to get out of the car and go to the craft. It was irresistible. I opened the door and started walking toward the craft while my folks frantically tried to call me back. Finally, my father got out of the car and held me. I became somewhat disoriented, and I think I experienced some time loss.

When we met up with Bob's family back at the campsite, we saw a large metallic disk hovering near the other side of the lake. Bob and his father ran toward it, yelling. The disk backed off, then disappeared with a brilliant flash and an explosion.

Suddenly, a very large booth, with a door and windows, appeared over the center of the lake. Bob's father was inside it. None of us could understand how he got there. As the large booth hovered motionless above us, a beam of pure blue light descended into the water in front of us. My father started wading into the lake to help Bob's father. About 40 feet in, the blue beam hit my father and he disappeared.

My mother herded me and my two sisters into the car. We sped off around the bay. From there we could still see the booth. We could also hear my father and Bob's father yelling and talking with an unseen voice, about what "they" wanted from Bob's father. It seemed that "they" were admonishing the two men about their responsibilities as wildlife conservation officers. We just sat there in the car until the booth was no longer illuminated.

As we drove slowly back to the campsite, we saw the dark form of the booth still hovering above the lake. After we got out of the car, my father came wading out of the lake, as if he had just appeared from nowhere. My sisters and I were very excited, but my parents seemed confused. They sent us to bed and told us to forget what we had seen.

We didn't see Bob's family until the next morning. By then, we all had mysteriously forgotten the entire affair — until 36 years later, when I had my flood of recollections.

Bob doesn't remember the Memphis Lake experience, but he recalls another similar encounter we had together. His father, who has since died, also remembered the beginning of that encounter, but he thought the craft had been a helicopter. Both of my sisters consider UFOs to be Satanic, so they won't talk to me about it. My parents have died and the others remember nothing.

— *John Foster, Lincoln, Nebraska*
August 1997

Its Face Was Green

My father, Louis Virden, was a master sergeant in the Signal Corp. In 1943, he was transferred from Texas to a post near Hattiesburg, Mississippi. He and my mother, Maurine, my brothers Louis (age 12) and George (six), and I (nine) lived in quarters provided for army families. There we settled down to what was considered a normal life during the war years. However, a few months later an event occurred that was anything but normal.

In the middle of a cold November night, Mother's hysterical screams awakened us. Our father was on duty and we three boys tried to calm her, but she kept sobbing and saying, "His face was green, green, I tell you!"

As we tried to ask her, "Whose face?" the thunder of a 12-gauge shotgun shattered the air. We ran into the chill night to find our next-door neighbor, a bald-headed man named Sergeant Thorne, holding the still-smoking gun. He had fired at what he assumed was an ordinary prowler and the cause of my mother's screams. He kept saying, "I hit him. I know I hit him square in the back, but he just kept on running!"

Someone came with a flashlight, and we all followed the path the intruder had taken to the highway that runs through McLauren. There on the asphalt were large splatters of yellow blood!

We began to believe something more than an ordinary prowler had startled my mother with his hideous green face. He had been able to run despite the full discharge of a 12-gauge shotgun in his back, and now, yellow blood! I think we children were no more scared than the adults.

Sergeant Thorne asked Mother, now somewhat calmer, how she had happened to see the intruder. She shoved her three chattering pajama-clad boys into the cabin, but through the thin walls we could hear her tell how it occurred.

She had been awakened by a loud pounding on the front door. She arose to answer, but when she drew aside the curtain to look out she saw no one. At that moment the knock sounded on the back door. Going to the rear entrance, she heard the loud knocking once more on the front door!

Thoroughly exasperated and thinking someone must be playing tricks on her, she ran to the front door once more and quickly drew back the curtain.

Through the window she saw not a human being but a manlike creature with a bright green face! The leering, other-worldly face had shocked her into hysterical screaming.

The alien "man" never was seen again. But the fear of him or his kind was felt throughout the small community for a long time afterward. Based on Mother's description and the testimony of those who saw the yellow blood, everybody believed our community had been visited by a being from some other world. To this day, when asked about that night, Mother will say in an awed tone, "His face was green, green, I tell you!"

— *J. Russell Virden, Arcadia, California*
February 1970

Return of the Green-Eyed Monster

My three daughters attended Dunedin Middle School in the 1960s, and I was divorced and working out of my garage as a sign painter — partly so I could keep an eye on the eight to 12 teenagers who would come over on Saturday nights to watch "Shock Theater."

The local police didn't like boys who owned cars to socialize in vacant parking lots, sitting on cars, drinking Cokes and eating Twinkies. They were always told to "break it up" and sent home.

One balmy evening the leader of the pack pulled in and declared he'd found a place where the cops couldn't find them — an old, one-lane dirt road which is now the main artery between Dunedin and St. Petersburg.

All the kids piled into four cars and off they went. About an hour later the pack and its leader pulled into the yard in a panic.

The only one who talked was the leader. He showed me scratches on his metallic silver car's trunk, then asked to have a pencil and paper for each person, which I provided. They all drew the same figure — just like the one I had seen in a FATE article in the 1940s, drawn by an old prospector!

I cautioned the kids and told them how the prospector had dragged himself back to town with a horrible sunburn, and that he had eventually died after being close to that creature he had drawn.

I had two friends with me, so we all followed the kids to the dirt road to see the beings. That was the start of a very strange two-week period in my life. We called the McGill Air Force Base in Tampa, but they wouldn't discuss it. No other parents would go to see the creatures, who would float from various pine trees along the road from 9:45 P.M. to 10:00 P.M., then disappear into a field where there was a herd of milk cows. We finally got a group of UFO watchers to witness the creatures, but none of them would get out of their cars.

The next night we had a sighting of three saucers. One was in the sky while another rose from the field, then another. The last one shot into the sky in a giant flame. All disappeared into the sky above the Gulf of Mexico.

I inquired if anyone else had seen this, and was told that a cow in the pasture had been turned into jelly and a woman became so hysterical she was rushed to a local sanatorium where it took her two weeks to recover. Happily, this time the kids were very careful and no one got hurt — although we were all kidded about our "green-eyed monsters" for a long time.

— *Grace Kerin, Dunedin, Florida*
June 1992

An Alien Named Gordon

Always a skeptic, I never believed UFOs existed because I'd never seen one. But I was willing to change my mind if one ever should show itself to me. After a harrowing drive over hundreds of miles of the Alaska Highway in October 1974 with my friend Nuria Hanson, I am a skeptic no longer.

Nuria and I had been attending a convention of the Coptic Christian Fellowship of America in Kalamazoo, Michigan. Hamid Bey, leader of the Fellowship in this country, had given me a blessing for the journey home, saying, "Guide her, protect her, and allow her to see your light."

As we drove the 1,500 miles home to Anchorage, the weather grew worse. After we passed Fort Nelson, British Columbia, the road became icy and a heavy fog cut visibility to a few yards. The nearest lodge was 30 miles away and we looked forward to a rest. I felt as if I had been fighting the car every mile, up and down steep hills and around sharp curves, all the while fearful that we might slide off the mountain road.

Then we noticed a light that we at first thought was a beacon for airplanes on the side of a mountain. The light moved toward us in an oscillating motion until it hovered between us and the mountainside; it was now about three times the size of the full moon. As it hovered, we knew it could not be a plane, or even a helicopter. It reminded us of a derby hat, with portholes all around it near the "brim." We could even make out the domed top, which was not lighted but which we could see from the reflected light of the portholes.

"Wow!" I exclaimed. "That's got to be a flying saucer, Nuria!"

We watched it for a long time before resuming our journey. Suddenly, I noticed that the car wasn't fighting me anymore. In fact, I wasn't driving it — it was driving itself! I took both hands off the wheel, but only an inch so that Nuria wouldn't notice. The car steered itself around curves without any help from me. I also found I couldn't alter the car's speed no matter how hard I stepped on the accelerator.

Finally, Nuria noticed and said, "If you don't have to steer the car, why don't you just put your hands in your lap?"

I did. The speed stayed the same and the car continued to negotiate curves without difficulty. It didn't even seem strange to us. A kind of pleasant, peaceful calm had settled in our minds. A light seemed to surround the car and when we rolled down our windows and put our heads out to look up, we saw the prettiest, fluffiest white cloud we had ever seen. Light emanated from it. We decided the UFO we had seen must be guiding us, protecting us, and driving the car. It all seemed a nice and pleasant thing; how very kind of them, we thought.

Eventually, we stopped at a lodge near Muncho Lake to stretch our legs. As we were getting back in, a dark-haired, bearded young man came striding up to us from the direction of the road.

"If you're going on, how are the chances of getting a ride with you?" he asked.

"I'm afraid there's no room," I said. "You can see the back of the car is loaded with luggage and we have only bucket seats in front — just room for the two of us."

It didn't occur to either Nuria or me to ask where he'd come from, why he was dressed only in a shirt and slacks without an overcoat or hat, or why he wore no boots or galoshes over his ordinary oxford-style shoes. The temperature was only a few degrees above zero and snow covered the ground at that elevation.

I asked him how far he was going.

"Just to the next lodge," he said, explaining that he worked there. "It's only about 80 miles."

I said, "The only way is for Nuria to sit on your lap or for you to sit on hers. If you want to do that we can give you a lift."

He said that would be fine. To my surprise he sat on Nuria's lap rather than suggesting she sit on his, as most men would have. But it would not be long before I understood why he acted as he did.

Since he was quite tall and there wasn't much headroom, we started that 80-mile stretch with him hunched over on Nuria's lap. He reminded me of someone, I kept thinking. Nuria thought the same thing, she told me later. But I didn't have time to question him at that moment because I had to concentrate on driving.

After a time I asked the young man what his name was.

He leaned forward and gazed intently into my eyes for several seconds. Then he said, "My name is Gordon." The significance of that name did not strike me until later.

After about five miles Nuria cleared her throat and asked Gordon, "How come I don't feel you?"

"What do you mean?"

"Gordon! You've been sitting on my lap for four or five miles now and you don't weigh anything! How come?"

"Oh," he laughed, "I'm very light. I don't weigh much at all. It's just your imagination that I don't weigh anything."

Incredible as it now seems, we both accepted that explanation as adequate. But I thought he must be mighty uncomfortable in that position and said so. He insisted he was fine.

I told him he would be more comfortable if he sat on the console between the two bucket seats. I reached behind the console and brought up a pillow.

Placing the pillow on the console I urged him to sit there where he could rest more easily. He did so, positioning himself so that an arm rested on the back of the seat behind each of us.

Soon after that I noticed the UFO light off to the left of us — the same one we had seen in the sky.

"Hey, Nuria!" I said. "There's our 'star' again."

She said we should stop and watch it to see what it was up to this time. Both of us got out but Gordon stayed in the car. The light was stationary, just below the tops of some trees. Suddenly it moved forward very rapidly and stopped.

Wanting confirmation of what we had seen I turned to Gordon and said, "There! You saw that, didn't you? Did that light move or didn't it?"

"Well, either the light moved," he joked, "or else the trees jumped up in front of it and then settled down again."

As we drove on and we told him all we had seen that night.

"Do you believe there are such things as what you call flying saucers?" he asked. "Do you believe there's life in the universe other than on this planet?"

"I didn't believe for sure until tonight," I told him, "but now that we've seen them, I know they exist. As for life elsewhere, we would be foolish to think we are unique in the whole universe."

Next Gordon wanted to know if we believed in angels. "What do you think they look like?" he asked. "Do you think they appear with halos and feathered wings?"

We replied that we certainly do believe in guiding angels, whatever one chooses to call them. "But as to appearance," I said, "well, you know the Bible warns us not to turn anyone away because we may be 'entertaining angels unawares.' After all, if some dude came up to you with a halo and wings, you'd be very well aware it was an angel. Probably the pictures people drew long ago showing them with wings were done to indicate angels came from the sky. So I think angels probably appear as very ordinary persons."

"You know," Gordon said, "you're right on all counts. Anyone who helps his fellow man, after all, is an angel."

As our journey continued I gradually became aware of something else that was strange. I couldn't figure out exactly what it was, but I eventually realized what bothered me about Gordon. He wasn't sitting on the pillow — he was sitting a few inches above it!

Alarmed, I felt under him with my hand to see if my impression was correct. Sure enough, I could run my hand between him and the pillow, touching the pillow but not him. He seemed not to notice.

Still unable to grasp the situation, I assumed that he must be holding himself up with his arms, which were resting on the backs of the seats.

"You must be terribly uncomfortable holding yourself up that way," I remarked.

"I assure you, I'm perfectly comfortable," Gordon insisted.

"But your arms must be aching after all this time in that position."

"Okay, if you insist," he said. And with that he took his arms off the seat backs and folded his hands in his lap without sinking down onto the pillow.

I was terror-struck. I desperately wanted to shout, scream, yell for help. I gasped for breath and nearly strangled in my fear. But before I could utter a sound, Gordon suddenly leaned forward, peered into my eyes, and said slowly, intently, distinctly, "Really, I'm perfectly all right. Please don't worry about me anymore."

Somehow that calmed me. The whole puzzle faded as if it were without significance. I didn't remember it until many hours later.

Gordon made us promise that when we arrived at the next lodge, Fireside Inn, we would stay there the rest of the night. He said the road beyond that point was too dangerous to drive.

Of course, we promised. It seemed natural to agree with him. He also insisted that we promise to do no more night driving the rest of the trip. We agreed to that too. He had warned us that while we would find the lodge open, we would be unable to book a room at that hour. He told us that we could sleep in the lobby until the lodge officially opened at 7:00 A.M.

We arrived at Fireside Inn at about 4:00 A.M., 165 miles from where we had stopped to watch the UFOs. We got out of the car and Nuria and I turned toward the lodge. Gordon got out behind me, Nuria and I turned back to get our purses, lock up the car, and thank Gordon for his help, but he wasn't there! I couldn't have glanced toward the lodge for more than a few seconds. Nuria said he was standing behind me one second and was gone the next. He did not get back into the car.

We searched in vain. A fresh snow had fallen but we saw no tracks. No footprints led away from the car in any direction. Nevertheless, Nuria walked out to the highway calling his name. I walked to each side of the lodge calling him. The only tracks in the fresh snow were ours.

Inside the lodge, the only other person in the lobby was a truck driver who dozed in an overstuffed chair. He woke when he heard us come in, and he said we were the first to enter in several hours.

When he told us we could not possibly have come all the way from Steamboat Mountain in the fog and ice, we naïvely told him everything that had happened.

That was a mistake. He hooted in derision. "You can't fool me with a bunch of lies like that!" he snorted. We realized then that we had better not tell anyone else our story.

Somehow we were not terribly disturbed about Gordon's disappearance. Perhaps we were just more tired than we realized. In any event we concluded that whatever had happened to Gordon, he was able to take care of himself. Finding a corner for each of us to curl up in, we wrapped up in the blankets we'd brought from the car and dozed for a few hours. When the manager arrived in the morning we rented a room for a few hours of more restful sleep.

Later we spent several hours discussing everything in detail. We couldn't believe how accepting we had been. Why had we not questioned Gordon? Where had he come from? Why was he dressed as he was? Why was he weightless? Was Gordon real, or a thought projection beamed at us from the UFOs? Was he a figment of our imaginations, a hallucination we both experienced? Where did he go when he left? Had Gordon controlled our thoughts, or read our minds? What happened when he peered so intently into our eyes?

Then I remembered who he reminded me of: my husband Jim! Nuria agreed. Gordon had Jim's hair color, eyes, build, beard, and mannerisms. And was it only coincidence that he said his name was "Gordon" — Jim's middle name. He had stared at me a bit before coming up with that name. Could he have taken it from my subconscious? If indeed he was some sort of thought projection, astral projection, or imaginary being beamed at us by a UFO, did he resemble Jim so that we would more readily accept him?

I remembered Hamid Bey's special blessing for the trip. He had petitioned for guidance and protection, and asked that I might see the light. We wondered if he had had anything to do with the appearance of the UFOs.

We remembered other things too. When the three of us had discussed UFOs, I said I wished they'd just pick us up, transport us to Anchorage, and be done with it. But Gordon had said, "Well, you wouldn't want to leave your car here, would you?"

"Oh no," I said. "My husband wouldn't understand that."

"Well, I think they wouldn't be able to take the car too," he had replied. "There would not be enough room. There's a reason for everything, remember, and sometimes you must continue doing certain things, like completing this trip, for the learning experiences that may be involved."

I remembered that when "Gordon" had taken his arm down from the back of the seat behind me he didn't do it in the way one would expect. He just sort of dragged his arm off the back of the seat to his lap without bending his elbow, leaning the other way or making the usual moves.

In other words, he must have dragged his arm and hand right through my shoulder!

The white cloud followed us for the remainder of our trip until we were four blocks from my home at about 5:00 A.M. October 22. Then the light blinked off and on again three times before sailing in a huge arc through the southern skies and zooming out to become one with the stars. It had moved directly in front of us before that final maneuver.

That seemed a spectacular and fitting farewell from Gordon or from "them." Whoever Gordon is or whatever "they" are, we appreciated the help. Nuria and I believe they'll be back somewhere, sometime, to help others just as they helped us from October 18 through October 22, 1974. Perhaps other people are being helped right now.

After all, Gordon had told us, "In the near future everyone will be seeing them, just as you have."

— *Edmoana Toews, as told to Joseph Brewer, Anchorage, Alaska*
June 1977

CREEPY CREATURES

Standing in the doorway was a little man about my height, stooped and leaning heavily on a gnarled cane. He was dressed in a tall, white hat, a white tuxedo-like suit and a white cape. His face was wrinkled and angry looking, his hair long, white and slightly curled, his hands crippled with work or disease, his nails very long. He grimaced and showed ragged, fang-like teeth. Everything about him seemed to shimmer and glow.
   — From Eva Pashke's "The Little Man in White," page 219

They only seem to be the stuff of late night horror movies — red-eyed demons, fanged gnomes, giant toads — yet hundreds of rational individuals have encountered creatures similar to those presented in this chapter. Our fascination with the unknown, the abnormal, the grotesque, and the dangerous has driven us to search for real-life monsters, and has resulted in the discovery of the Komodo dragon, giant squid, and coelacanth, among other zoological oddities. Perhaps our fears are based on more than old folktales and horror movies.

King of the Toads

In the 1930s the little town of Verona, New Jersey, was a pleasant place of woods and meadows for children like me to wander through. I became familiar with many facets of nature but the tale told to my mother and me by a neighbor has remained a mystery until this day.

Mrs. Inhalt lived across the street from us with her son William and his wife. All were highly respected, hardworking people of German extraction, not given to flights of fancy. Although we children spoke of her as "old Mrs. Inhalt," in reality she probably was no more than 60 years old. This designator simply differentiated her from her daughter-in-law who had the same name. An avid flower gardener, old Mrs. Inhalt was delighted in the early spring of 1931 when my mother obtained a certain plant for her from an aunt in another town. Mrs. Inhalt promised to put it in the ground that very same afternoon.

We did not see her again for two or three weeks. When we discovered Mrs. Inhalt had not been feeling well Mother went over to visit and I tagged along. At first Mrs. Inhalt seemed to avoid questions about her illness but suddenly she seemed to make up her mind and told the following story:

"I went out to put your gift plant on the south side in the sunniest location," she told us, "and decided to place it in the grassy part by the field next door so it would have room to expand. This meant cutting out a section of the sod, so I lifted the shovel and brought it down with considerable force to cut through the grass and roots.

"Just as I drove it down, I saw too late to stop that my shovel was aimed directly at a large brown toad that was concealed in the dried brownish grass. The blade of the shovel cut off both of the poor creature's legs and I could do nothing but watch in sick horror as he twitched and bled to death.

"I would not knowingly harm a living thing and I was unable to move for shock. I stood staring down for several minutes until I became aware of the feeling I was in danger. I looked around but saw no one and then realized I was surrounded by little brown toads. There were hundreds of them sitting in a circle looking at me and in the grass farther out I could see more and more of them, all coming quickly from every direction. None were as large as the dead toad; it was at least twice their size.

"I don't know what might have happened but I threw down my shovel and ran into the house. The incident so upset me that I was overcome by nausea and headache and remained in bed for several days.

"When Bill came home from work," Mrs. Inhalt concluded, "I told him about the toads. He looked in the garden but found only your plant, which he put in the ground for me. The shovel was lying there with a stain on the tip but there was no sign of the dead toad or any other. I never have seen a toad in the garden before and I hope I never see another."

In all our years of wandering the fields and forests we neighborhood children were quite familiar with frogs, snakes, polliwogs, crawfish and other living things but I probably had seen fewer than a half dozen toads.

We never were able to explain what happened when Mrs. Inhalt killed the giant toad. Her own expression, all the more startling coming from so practical a person, was that she had killed the king of the toads and the others came in response to a message she could not hear. I still wonder why that one toad was so much larger than the others, why hundreds of small toads came when he died and what would have happened to Mrs. Inhalt had she not run into the house.

> — *Susan R. Treidel, New Orleans, Louisiana*
> *August 1975*

The Red-Eyed Creature

I n 1985, two of my friends, Chris Caballero and Tony Anderson, and I lived in a house on San Antonio's East Side. We were sitting around one night after moving in with the help of Patrick Najera, who lived nearby with his grandparents. His grandparents had found the house for us. Our friend Vicki Germaine was also visiting.

It was almost Halloween, so we decided to tell scary stories by candlelight. We turned the lights off and lit candles. Patrick started to tell us how nearly everyone in the neighborhood avoided the house, but he didn't know why. Vicki suddenly screamed, "There's something with red eyes in the kitchen!"

We thought she was putting us on, and we laughed it off. From what we could see of the kitchen through the open door, it was empty. Tony got up to go to the bathroom, which was next to the kitchen. As he walked by the kitchen door he shouted, "There is something in there!" He threw a chair, but it came back, landing at his feet. He closed the door. Tony insisted that the chair had stopped in midair before flying back, untouched by anything he could see. Both Tony and Vicki insisted that the presence in the kitchen wasn't human, that it had red eyes, and that it looked like a gargoyle. We stayed up all night, afraid to sleep.

The next day I went with Patrick to his grandparents' house. We asked his grandmother, Mrs. Najera, if she knew anything about the house's past. She told us there had been nothing unusual until about five years ago, when the young girl who lived there had been hit by a car in front of the house and died. After her death, people began to report that they had seen a strange creature around the house.

Shortly after this creature began to appear, a mysterious fire burned the kitchen and the family who had been living there moved out. The house had been vacant until we moved in. Until we moved out, each of us saw the creature at least once. Usually it stood over us as we slept. It never did any harm. It just seemed to be watching, or perhaps even protecting.

— *Alton Carroll, San Antonio, Texas*
April 1995

The Talking Tom Cat

At age nine, I lived in north Georgia. While I was waiting for the school bus one morning, a large yellow tom cat walked right past me and planted himself on our front porch. When I got home from school he was sitting in the same spot, waiting. I fed him and dubbed him Tom. A week later we moved to the country and Tom came with us.

The cat was so gentle — he would sleep in my lap and curl his tail around so he could suck it like a baby. But he was also my staunchest defender. When my mother and I took night walks, Tom would walk a few feet ahead of us, stopping only when we stopped. When I began to sleepwalk, he was always with me, though I didn't know it until I awoke. He defended me from snakes, rats, and even a German Shepherd attack. But I never realized what a guardian he was until one night when my parents and I were watching television in the den.

That evenning we heard strange noises, like voices coming from the basement. Tom stood before the basement door, growling, his hair on end. My father went to the door and opened it. The voices were louder. My father yelled that he had a gun, which wasn't true.

Tom walked around him, crouched, and growled into the dark as he crawled slowly down the stairs. As we watched, Tom went halfway down and stopped. As he did, the voices stopped, too. Then from Tom's mouth came something I'll never forget: His growling noises became strained words that sounded to all of us like, "Get out ... No, I won't let you ... No, I won't do it!"

Terrified, my father called to him. Tom turned, green eyes glowing and claws out, and jumped straight to my father's chest. My father screamed and threw Tom aside.

That night, Tom slept in front of the basement door, still on guard. The basement had a small room, filled to the ceiling with soil. I always wondered what was under that dirt.

Four years later, I went away and my parents moved. We never saw Tom again.

— *Barbara Healy, Belleville, Illinois*
December 1996

The Little Man in White

When I was eight years old, we moved to a large house in Freeport, Illinois. That winter in 1906 was cold and my older stepsister, Dell, developed a bad case of pleurisy.

My stepmother was exhausted from trying to keep house and nurse Dell, so my father moved her to the bedroom downstairs where it was warmer. He brought down two huge feather beds and put them on the floor. He told my sister Marcie, 11 years old, my stepsister Ethel, 13 years old, and me to sleep in the same room with Dell and to call him if there was any change in her condition.

The first thing we did after we were certain our parents were in the kitchen was to get into a pillow fight.

Suddenly Dell sat up in bed and started to sing "And Her Name Was Rose," at the top of her voice. We stopped the pillow fight at once. Dell turned, still singing and evidently delirious, toward the door leading into the darkened living room. We turned too.

Standing in the doorway was a little man about my height, stooped and leaning heavily on a gnarled cane. He was dressed in a tall, white hat, a white tuxedo-like suit and a white cape. His face was wrinkled and angry looking, his hair long, white and slightly curled, his hands crippled with work or disease, his nails very long. He grimaced and showed ragged, fang-like teeth. Everything about him seemed to shimmer and glow.

Suddenly Ethel began screaming and Marcie and I joined in. The little man raised his cane, shook it and started in our direction. We heard a shout from the kitchen and my father burst into the room. I was looking at the little man and he vanished instantly.

Dell fell back on the bed. She went into a deep sleep and in a few days was well again. Although my father inquired, no one in Freeport knew of any explanation for the little man and we never saw him again.

— Eva Pashke, Chicago, Illinois
December 1957

Of Fairies and Gnomes

I was in the garden with my mother at her home called "Highways," on Wells Road in Somerset, England, when this occurred. Mother wanted to show me the correct way the take cuttings from rose trees. She stood behind the finest rose tree we had with a pair of scissors in her hand, while I stood in front of it. Thus we faced one another with the rose tree between us.

Suddenly Mother put a finger to her lips to indicate silence and then pointed to one of the blooms. With astonishment I saw what she was seeing — a little figure about six inches high, in the perfect shape of a woman and with brilliantly colored diaphanous wings resembling those of a dragonfly. The figure held a little wand and was pointing it at the heart of a rose. At the tip of the wand there was a little light, like a star. The figure's limbs were a very pale pink and visible through her clothes. She had long silvery hair that resembled an aura. She hovered near the rose for at least two minutes, her wings vibrating rapidly like those of a hummingbird, and then she disappeared.

"You saw that, didn't you?" asked my mother. I nodded and we both went back to the house astonished and enriched by our mutual experience and having forgotten entirely our rose-cutting.

Perhaps the most surprising aspect of the experience was the way in which the little creature we both saw corresponded in practically every detail to the archetypal fairy of folklore and nursery stories. I know now that these descriptions are firmly founded on reality.

This was proven to me once again by a second experience I had when I was alone in the same garden. I was sitting reading under a tree when my eye was caught by a sudden movement in front of me. A little figure, about 18 inches tall, ran from the lawn on my left, across a path and onto another lawn, finally disappearing under a young fir tree. The sturdily built figure seemed to be dressed in a brown one-piece suit. I was not able to see the face because it was turned away from me. I immediately jumped up to investigate the area around the fir tree but there was no longer any sign of this gnome.

Not long after this episode a friend of the family, who was obliging my mother by digging in the vegetable garden, saw the same gnome and described it to me.

In the past, great scholastic theologians such as Thomas Aquinas, Bonventura and Albertus Magnus believed that demons were able to form physical bodies from the air, the earth and waters and in these bodies they could have intercourse with mortal women. However ridiculous this idea may appear in our age, it does prove that those learned doctors of the thirteenth century knew of the existence of superworlds and accepted as true the folklore of their times, of which gnomes, undines, sylphs and salamanders were a part.

Gervase of Tilbury, who died in 1235, in his story entitled "De Antipodibus et Eorum Terra," speaks of fairyland and its people. Virgilius, Bishop of Salzburg, was condemned by Pope Zacharias in the Eighth Century for his doctrine concerning a subterranean world in which there is a sun, a moon and tiny creatures resembling men. St. Godric, a twelfth-century hermit, claimed that a male fairy appeared to him and asked him for some apples but then threw away the apples that Godric gave him and promptly disappeared, leaving behind "an unspeakable odor" which made the saint's "hair stand on end." These citations are merely a random selection from a vast and fascinating treasure-house of "submerged tradition" which has yet to be collected and reduced to order. If this is undertaken the resultant picture of evolving human beliefs will be very different from the one presented by self-conscious churchianity.

We may be able to look forward to a time when gnomes, undines, sylphs, and salamanders will be accepted as easily as findings about the atom, the genetic structure of human beings and the possibility of life on other planets.

— *Cynthia Monteflore, Bath, Avon, England*
May 1977

The Werewolf of Greggton

A strange experience happened to me one night last July in 1958, when my husband was away on business. I had pushed my bed close to a large window hoping to catch the cool breeze from a thunder storm which was gathering on the southwestern horizon. It was stifling hot and I couldn't seem to rest. But I snapped off the bed light and lay quietly trying to go to sleep.

Finally I dozed off. How long I slept I do not know, but I awakened with a start. A faint scratching sound was coming from the screened window beside my face. I lay still staring at the screened window as the seconds ticked by. Suddenly a bright flash of lightning lit up the window for an instant. I grasped in horror. A huge, shaggy, wolf-like creature was clawing at the screen and glaring at me with baleful, glowing, slitted eyes. I could see its bared white fangs.

I grabbed my flashlight from the night table nearby and leaped from the bed. Then I shot the beam of light toward the window in time to catch another glimpse of the monstrous animal as it fled away from the open window, across the yard into a thick clump of bushes near the highway.

I watched for the animal to come out of the bushes but, after a short time, instead of a great shaggy wolf running out, the figure of an extremely tall man suddenly parted the thick foliage and walked hurriedly off down the road, disappearing into the darkness.

Cold prickles of fear ran over me. I closed the window and locked it. I slept with a bright light on in my room the rest of that night.

— *Mrs. Delburt Gregg, Greggton, Texas*
March 1960

GHOST STORIES

We looked and clearly saw a man, fully dressed, hanging by a rope.
A few minutes later the figure vanished.
— *Dr. C. A. Hill, "The Man in the Doorway," page 230*

Nearly everyone likes a good ghost story, perhaps because we have walked carefully through a graveyard or an old unlighted building and had the feeling that we're not alone. FATE magazine has received more letters from readers about ghostly encounters than any other paranormal phenomenon. People have sensed the presence of deceased friends, family, pets — or in cases such as Dr. Hill's, complete strangers. Some of the spirits have arrived in the guise of guardian angels. Others have had more sinister intentions. But most of them have merely appeared and disappeared, enigmatically providing a brief glimpse of the future that awaits us all.

The Trunk in the Attic

In death, Ranee Stanton was the same as she'd been in life — cold, selfish, and cruel — especially to her daughter, Doris, who had devoted her life to caring for her mother. From the day her daughter came into the world, old Mrs. Stanton had been determined her child would stay with her. Throughout the years, she told Doris about the wicked ways of men, using Doris' own father as an example.

Jerold Stanton had left them when Doris was only six months old, leaving Ranee to bring up the child alone. Doris had once seen a photo of her father and thought he seemed kindly, but this could not be true. She never had any personal contact with her father, but her mother had often told Doris that he had never shown the slightest bit of interest in his daughter.

At the tender age of 18, Doris met and fell in love with Frank Burrows, to Ranee's horror. Coincidentally, it was around this time that old Mrs. Stanton developed severe angina attacks and demanded constant attention from her daughter.

Frank never liked his girlfriend's mother. He could see through her play-acting — the sudden attacks that occurred just as he and Doris were about to go out, with the old woman's voice calling after them, "Go out, leave me alone, and don't expect me to be alive when you get back!" It amazed Frank that Doris could not see through her mother's games.

"Please," pleaded Doris. "Be patient with Mother. She'll come around in time." But she never did and three years later Frank gave Doris the ultimatum: "Leave with me now or we're finished." Doris was loyal to her mother. To leave her alone was out of the question.

The years passed and she remained in love with Frank. Forty years later she was devastated when she learned that he had died in Australia. Her mother had also somehow learned of Frank's death. Ranee told her daughter, "If you had wed him you would have been left a widow alone in a strange country."

"I may not have been alone, Mother," whispered Doris. "Maybe I'd have my own family, even grandchildren. Best of all, I would have had 40 years of happiness with Frank."

"Don't talk foolish, girl," roared Ranee, still speaking to her as if she were 10 years old. "He was no good. Couldn't wait for you, could he? Never wrote once to you from Australia, did he? Out of sight, my girl, and out of mind."

Doris knew this was true, but she felt the tears sting as they rolled down her face, and she cried for what might have been.

At the grand old age of 84, Ranee really did fall ill. "A massive stroke," the doctor said as he wrote out the death certificate.

The old woman had been buried about a week when Doris started having nightmares. Night after night, the same dream haunted her sleep.

In each of the dreams she found herself in the attic with an old trunk. Upon opening it, Ranee's face jumped out, glared angrily at Doris, and warned her not to took inside and meddle in things that did not concem her.

Months passed. At first, Doris was afraid of living alone. In all her 60-odd years Mother had always been there. Mother had made all the decisions, but now it was finally up to Doris to make her own.

In less than a year she would be retiring from her job. She welcomed the change because the last 10 years had been difficult. In fact, she would have changed jobs, but her mother had always persuaded her not to.

Doris made her first major decision — to sell the house where she had grown up and move into an apartment. After all, on such a small pension she would not be able to afford the upkeep for the old, two-bedroom cottage.

On a Friday she called a real estate agent from work and made arrangements for him to come by on Monday aftemoon, which would give her ample time to straighten things up over the weekend.

After work, Doris began the task of sorting. The first job would have to be the attic. She pulled down the foldaway steps and made her way up. The attic smelled musty and was cluttered with old boxes, unwanted pictures, and omaments. Then, in the far comer, she saw an old-fashioned metal trunk. Every hair on her body stood on end, for this was the trunk in her dreams. She retreated down the stairs, wishing she were brave enough to open the trunk. An hour later she was on the the phone asking for my help. Doris needed me to be with her when she opened the old trunk. She was afraid and it was too much for her to face alone.

Not sure about what to expect, I followed her up into the musty attic. In the far corner stood the mysterious old trunk.

"Would you like me to open it for you?" I asked, sensing her apprehension.

Her round face broke into a gentle smile. "Yes, please," she said.

Although I felt no presence or ghost in the room with us, I was still anxious, not because of Doris's mother, but because of the importance of this old trunk's contents. Why had Doris dreamed, night after night, that it should not be opened? What was her mother trying to warn her about? One thing was certain: We would soon find out.

Cautiously I lifted the lid, half expecting Doris' mother to jump out at me. We were surprised to find only letters, hundreds of them, all addressed to Doris. Bundled together with rubber bands, the opened letters were carefully stacked.

"My darling Doris,

"My illness is getting worse; steadily I'm growing weaker. If only you would acknowledge my letters. I love you. My love will never die. Please write this time, Doris, please write."

The signature was Frank's. From the look on Doris' shocked face, it was obvious she had never seen these letters.

"All these years, I have loved Frank, thinking he had forgotten me and married someone else. All these years Mother knew. She took my letters, and never told me. All these years he kept writing. Even in death she tried to stop me from finding them. Frank cared after all. He never forgot me. But it's too late for us now, its too late!"

Doris sobbed uncontrollably.

There was nothing I could say to console her, feeling her sorrow as we carried the bundles of letters down to the sitting room. At Doris' request, I left her alone to read the letters in private.

The next day, Doris gave me a call. "It's Mother. She's come back. She's angry the trunk was opened."

Doris sounded so distressed that I drove over to see her. The icy presence that met me on my arrival at the cottage was Ranee Stanton's ghost.

The old woman had returned, her ghostly presence still showing no sign of remorse, no apology. She only had words of criticism: "Tell Doris it's her own fault. I told her not to open the trunk."

"But the letters were for your daughter. You had no right to withhold them from her," I said angrily.

"If she'd known Frank was still in love with her she would have left me and gone off with him to live in Australia. What would I have done then?" Mrs. Stanton's ghost snapped.

"Survived, Mrs. Stanton. Survived," I replied.

My remark must have angered her because the kitchen clock fell from the wall and missed me by a fraction of an inch. Doris's mother was the same as she had always been, selfish and self-centered.

Thankfully she left us alone for the rest of the afternoon. Before leaving, Doris promised to inform me if her mother appeared again.

About a week later, I dreamed of Doris. She was wearing a long white dress, like a bride, and her eyes were smiling at me. She looked very happy as she told me that she was going to marry Frank. "I've just come to say goodbye and to thank you for your help," she said.

The dream disturbed me to such an extent that when I woke up I drove to her cottage. She wasn't home so I pushed a note through her letter box asking her to call me as soon as possible. No call came. Her neighbor sent me the news of how she'd been rushed to the hospital the night before, where she died of a heart attack.

Later I also learned that Doris' father had never abandoned the family; it had been Ranee who had walked out on the marriage, taking her baby daughter with her. Throughout Doris' childhood, her father had tried to see her numerous times, only to be told by his ex-wife that his daughter was a serious asthmatic and upset could kill her. Doris never suffered from any form of asthma — this was simply another tale. Jerold Stanton had sent money for his daughter every Christmas and every birthday up until he died. Doris never knew.

Doris' mother had controlled her daughter's life for decades, but at last Doris had a chance for happiness. Mrs. Stanton prevented her daughter from marrying Frank in life but, thankfully, she could not prevent it in death.

— *Tarona Gail Hawkins*
October 1996

The Disappearing Hitchhiker

I was waiting for a traffic light when I saw the girl. She was hitch-hiking and both her raised thumb and her wistful look said that she wanted to ride with me.

"No," I muttered to myself as the light changed to green, "no time tonight."

Anyway, I thought, she would probably have to go to some out-of-the-way place, since no one could want to go the route I intended to take.

So, with a sheepish feeling and eyes downcast to miss her gaze, I whizzed through the intersection. I made good time on my way across town, and soon came out on the freeway at the point where I had planned. As I slowed to take my place in the traffic, I saw the same girl again! There she stood, with the same wistful look and the same raised-thumb signal.

This time I stopped. In a moment she was in. I mumbled some incoherent things about having passed her the first time. Finally I stammered, "How far are you going? I turn off at Avenue 64." Through the traffic noise I gathered that this was fine with her.

Then I began to think: How could this girl have arrived at the freeway before me? It was eight miles from where I had seen her before, and no other motorist could have given her a ride and reached the freeway before me. I had taken every short cut and driven over the speed limit.

I decided to ask my passenger some questions, but first I had to give my full attention to my driving as we went through a crowded, difficult curve. When I turned to talk to my passenger, she was gone.

We had been traveling at 60 miles per hour on a crowded three-lane freeway. One moment I had a pretty, young girl sitting beside me. The next, the seat was empty.

— *Chester E. Hall, Los Angeles, California*
December 1961

The Man in the Doorway

Some 30 years ago my father, a government man, was transferred to Jamestown, New York. We rented a small house which recently had been vacated. My sister, Lucille, 15, my brother, Frank, 14, and I, 12, were left alone in the house one cold November evening while my parents attended a lecture at the high school.

After they had left we three children sat in the dark in front of the fireplace awaiting their return. Time passed and suddenly, Lucille exclaimed as she looked toward the entrance door, "Look at that man hanging in the doorway!"

We looked and clearly saw a man, fully dressed, hanging by a rope. A few minutes later the figure vanished. Hurriedly putting on our coats, we rushed out of the house toward the high school to meet our parents. We met them coming home and, when we told them what we had seen, Father reprimanded us. After a sound spanking we were sent to bed.

The following evening, while conversing with Father, the neighbor next door offhandedly said he had seen us children leaving the house the night before. Father laughed and explained why.

The neighbor replied, "You need not laugh. A short time before you moved into the house a man did hang himself over the door. That is the reason the house is vacant. If you will look over the door you will see the big spike he tied the rope to."

The nail was there.

Father apologized to us and added, "I just can't understand it."

— *Dr. C. A. Hill, Long Beach, California*
December 1957

Our Smelly Ghost

What happened to us in the house in Yucaipa, California, which we rented for six months in 1966, might not happen to other tenants so it would be unfair to its owner to disclose its exact location. For us, however, it was a haunted house filled with strange odors and an enervating force that sapped my wife's strength, a force which also affected other women who visited us.

Ina and I had been married in the spring and we felt it was a stroke of luck to find such a nice house completely furnished, especially when we learned the rent was well within our means. All we had to do was move in and this we did early in April. The small house had one bedroom, a large living room with a dining area at one end, a modern kitchen and a large screened-in porch off the kitchen.

We were delighted at first but after a few weeks Ina began to complain of lacking energy. Her daughter Tia and her sister Helen often visited us and after a short stay Helen would remark that she was very tired. No one could understand it. The feeling of weariness never seemed to affect the men who came to the house, only the women.

We had lived in the house about a month when Ina woke me one night and said she could smell cleaning fluid. Fearful of fire she insisted we search the house for the source of the odor. I could not detect the odor but I went along with her. She said it pervaded the whole house and when we could find no cause for it I suggested it might be coming from outside. We donned robes and went out but there Ina said the smell was gone. We made a complete circuit around the house but still she could not detect the odor. Once again inside it was as strong as ever.

This happened on several occasions and each time we searched but with no success. All this time only Ina smelled the cleaning fluid but then one night I too caught the scent. The next day I literally tore the house apart searching in vain for the source of the odor.

About two weeks after Ina began smelling the cleaning fluid she awakened one night and smelled cologne — a disagreeable experience for her because she does not like scent of any kind and owns neither cologne nor perfume. Again we arose and searched the house and since I had not smelled the cologne I thought it might be my shaving lotion.

"No," she said, "it's different."

Several times the cologne odor awakened her in the middle of the night. "It's always the same fragrance," she said. "But it's only in the bedroom — nowhere else in the house."

By September Ina was very tired. She said she felt as if something were draining her strength. Being awakened so frequently by these strange odors wasn't helping either. She decided to visit her sister for a week to see if she could get some rest.

When I was alone in the house I began to be awakened by strange odors. The second night Ina was gone I awoke to the smell of freshly ironed clothes although no ironing had been done since Ina left. I got up and searched the house again and found the odor strongest near the screened-in porch. Still I could find no reason for it.

The next night I smelled cleaning fluid. This time I didn't even bother to investigate. I had concluded it was useless. After that I was awakened every night until my wife returned by the odor of cleaning fluid or fresh ironing.

The first night Ina was back the odor of cologne awakened us both. This was the first time I had smelled the fragrance. It was very strong over the bed and grew fainter toward the edges of the room. It seemed as if someone wearing the cologne were leaning over the bed looking down at us. We both are very sensitive to this and will awaken almost immediately if it actually happens.

We concluded that it was happening and we decided to ignore whoever or whatever it was. Somehow we learned to go back to sleep. I think this made our "haunt" angry and led to the ensuing events.

One night we had retired and put out the light but we still were sitting up in bed talking drowsily. Suddenly Ina stiffened in terror. From her side of the bed she could see a mirror in the dining area in which the whole living room was visible in the dim light filtering in from the street. From my side of the bed I couldn't see the mirror but Ina was staring at it in horror. She grabbed my arm and screamed, "What was that? Who was that?"

After I managed to calm her down she told me what she had seen. While she looked into the mirror the form of an elderly woman materialized, apparently standing in the middle of the living room. No, it was no one she knew or even vaguely like any of her friends or relatives. When she collected her senses sufficiently she looked back at the mirror. The apparition had vanished.

We got out of bed and searched the house, of course finding no one. All the doors and windows were locked — but at the spot where Ina had said the apparition stood the odor of that now-familiar cologne was very strong.

The next day Ina's daughter came over and found her mother very upset. When Tia heard the story of events of the night before she went into the living room (which Ina that day preferred to stay out of) and found the heavy sweet odor still remained in the center of the room. She went to the windows and the smell was not there. She then told her mother, "You know, when I bring Aunt Helen over here, she always complains afterward of being extremely sleepy. She says the house makes her tired and she doesn't like it."

Now we thought we could understand why every woman who entered the house became so tired. The spirit was gathering energy from them and Ina was getting the worst of it because she was there all the time. As much as we liked the place we started talking about finding another house.

I was not fully ready to accept the reality of our unwelcome guest (or hostess) until I had my own experience with her. She didn't appear for me but she sat down on my side of the bed next to me. The bedclothes suddenly were pulled tight across me and I could not pull them loose. How could I find out what she wanted? No matter how I tried I couldn't seem to get through to her.

Finally I thought it was time to let her know where she stood. Aloud I said, "You may have frightened my wife but you don't frighten me one bit so you might as well leave!"

The tension on the bedclothes slackened and evidently she left. That night she didn't bother Ina at all and this was her last visit for a week. I thought we were rid of her for good but I soon learned she was only building up energy for another maneuver.

One morning Ina was sitting on the couch in the living room and I was on the floor at her feet. In the middle of a sentence she stopped talking and a strange expression came over her face. Slowly her features changed until she didn't look like my Ina. She spoke in a voice I never had heard before.

"I'm going to kill that silly little wife of yours."

"Why are you going to kill her?" I asked in surprise.

She replied, "Because I want her body, that's why."

"Who are you?"

"You know who I am," she countered.

Then I asked if she had been visiting us almost every night. She replied that she had but still refused to identify herself.

I was quite alarmed, for as much as I wanted to continue the contact with this being I was afraid of what it was doing to Ina. Suddenly, whoever or whatever had taken possession of her body left and Ina's face and voice returned to normal. She had no memory of the conversation when I reported it to her.

Only one indication that I had not imagined the whole thing remained. Ina's skin carried the odor of that cologne we so often had smelled in the house. No matter how often she bathed she could not rid herself of the scent.

That afternoon we started looking for another place to live. As soon as we had moved Ina became well and strong again and the detested odor of the cologne disappeared.

Now we know that the spirit was imprisoned in the house we left and could not follow us. Maybe she didn't like us anyway.

— *Ward A. Roy*
May 1970

The Midnight Hearse

My father Paul Shaw, a surveyor for H. M. Customs and Excise, was sent in 1906 to Ballyhaunis, a small town in western Ireland. He took with him his young English wife, as he often did on his frequent trips away from their home in Herne Bay, Kent, England.

Uncertain as to how long his mission in Ireland would last they took rooms in McCrory's Hotel, the one inn in the quiet little town, instead of renting a house. Life there was far from dull, they found. There were parties, dances and race meetings — and of course the long winter evenings around a cozy fire given over to story-telling.

My mother took a lively interest in the new country and its people but she was inclined to laugh off the tales of ghosts and spirits and supernatural happenings so enthusiastically embraced by the Irish.

Nevertheless, she herself on more than one occasion returning from a dance or party saw that horses would not cross a certain bridge outside Ballyhaunis. If forced they reared in terror. To lead the horses past the spot the men had to get out of the coach and blindfold them. It was commonly said the bridge was "haunted."

Mostly, however, Mother called the tall tales "Celtic twilight." Then one night about the middle of April she and my father retired early. It was an unseasonably muggy night and in the fashion of the times the room was almost hermetically sealed with heavy drapes and dark blinds at the windows. My father, after an exacting day, fell asleep promptly but Mother could not. As she lay beside him she suddenly heard a vehicle approaching — the steady clip-clop of horses, hooves, creaking carriage wheels, jingling harness sounding clearly across the utter and complete stillness of the sleeping town.

"Like a hearse," she thought.

She heard its steady advance. As the vehicle turned into the town square the noises became clearer. Then to her astonishment the horses halted before the hotel entrance. This was an irresistible temptation to my curious mother! She got out of bed, awakening my father at the same time, and padded in her bare feet to the window.

Pulling the blind aside she stared down at the street below. Bright moonlight illuminated the square. She saw a vast black coach, the coachman sitting motionless on his perch, whip held erect, and four black horses standing patiently between the shafts.

"What is it doing down there?" she wondered aloud.

"Whatever it is it's none of your business," my father said crossly. "Come back to bed at once."

She obeyed with reluctance but she confesses she must have fallen asleep very quickly for she heard no one leave the hotel to be driven away in the coach nor did she hear if someone alighted and entered the hotel.

The next morning she tripped downstairs determined to disregard Father's "stuffiness" and get to the bottom of this odd affair. What important guest had arrived at the hotel so late at night? She had seen the truly magnificent equipage which must have belonged to a person of rank and wealth.

Greeting Mrs. McCrory, the proprietor's wife, Mother asked innocently, "What was that huge black coach doing outside the hotel last night?"

Mrs. McCrory turned pale and hastily crossed herself. She muttered something unintelligible and hurriedly withdrew.

The McCrorys' inn was a modest family-run hotel and Mother had free run of it as a welcome guest. But now she felt a tension in the air. When she followed uninvited into the family's private quarters she halted on the threshold sensing for the first time that she was intruding.

The McCrory family was assembled in the living room, the parish priest was there and all were on their knees praying. Some of the elders were in tears. More puzzled than ever Mother sought out the oldest daughter, Eileen, with whom she had a firm friendship, and insisted on an explanation — which Eileen seemed strangely reluctant to give.

"Sure, 'tis only an old superstition," she said uneasily. "The death warning for the McCrorys."

Mother knew many Irish families of pure Milesian descent have their family forewarnings of sorrow — the banshee, sidhe or some other fairy. She realized the McCrorys must believe the great black coach she had reported seeing was a supernatural phenomenon and that to them it must represent a traditional family omen. She continued to question Eileen and learned that few persons ever saw it and some only heard it. It seemed extraordinary that someone of another nationality and family — an alien, so to speak — should have glimpsed the phantom.

For once Mother was tongue-tied.

Throughout the day there was much coming and going. Family members clustered behind closed doors speaking in hushed voices. Then, on the evening of April 20, 1906, Mother had a fresh sensation to ponder.

Ill tidings traveled slowly in those days; the English newspapers arrived late the day after they were published. And when they did come on the late train, their screaming headlines broke the news of the great San Francisco earthquake, April 18, 1906.

Three days later the McCrorys received a telegram they seemed to have been expecting. The body of their son, Andrew, who had been serving as a priest in California, had been found in the ruins left by the quake.

— *Maureen Wakefield*
June 1970

No Reflection

In July 1990, I worked the late shift as an armed security officer. I arrived home after work one night to find a note saying that my parents were out shopping. I greeted my lovable, fearless Yorkie, Molly Princess, and ate a frozen dinner before heading off to bed and settling down to sleep.

After what seemed like only a few minutes, I felt Molly climb onto the bed. She appeared to be trying to hide near me. She was trembling. As I was calming her, I saw a shadow cross in front of the door. Molly seemed frozen in place, staring at the door.

I was shocked to see the door swaying. Slowly, a figure came through the door.

First a finger, then a hand, then a wrist, a shoulder ... and finally, the most evil profile I could ever imagine — that of an old, bald man, with a long, hooked nose. He seemed to be completely black and two-dimensional.

I remember wondering why his figure was not reflected in my wall mirror.

For a reason I can't explain, he was the most evil thing I have ever seen. I remember shouting Jesus' name, then reaching for my service weapon. Though this took a second at most, when I tumed back the "shadow" was gone.

In a panic, I bolted to the door, pushed it open, and stood in the living room, looking for the shadow. The bathroom door creaked, and I turned to see the apparition disappear into the bathroom.

I closed the bathroom door, then guarded it until my parents returned. The shadow never re-emerged, and I haven't seen it again — but it haunts my dreams, and I often wonder if it visits my dog's dreams, too.

> — *John Tavares, New Bedford, Massachusetts*
> *January 1996*

The Uninvited Visitor

Back in 1941 I was residing in England. I had been asked by my husband's boss, Kenneth Bryson, to meet him regarding chemical formulas belonging to my husband, a research chemist. The firm had moved away from London. This necessitated my traveling about 40 miles west to a small country town, Oakham, where he was living in the former vicarage of a church about 400 years old.

After a nice dinner and a pleasant evening we retired to our respective bedrooms, which were next to each other. I cannot say how long it was before I went to sleep, but I was suddenly awakened by the door being opened, and an elderly lady dressed in clothes of the early Victorian era came toward my bed. As she drew nearer I began to get a choking feeling in my throat. She appeared to glide down my bed and up the other side, then bent over me while her blue eyes stared closely at me. With difficulty I gave a shout because I felt that someone was strangling me. She suddenly disappeared and the door slammed.

The next morning my host had to unjamb the door and on doing so he said he knew that I had experienced "it."

I told him what had happened and he said that at the turn of the century the Vicar's wife had been found strangled in the basement. The murderer had never been found and since then she comes back every time there is a stranger in the house to satisfy herself that it is not her killer. The local people stay away from the Vicarage but people, particularly from America, specifically come to share the experience. Fifty years later, it's still very clear in my mind!

— *Marjorie Philips, Sequel, California*
September 1991

The Spirit of Spiritualism

I was born in 1916 in Ponce, Puerto Rico. Early in life I began studying the paranormal through the books of Allan Kardek, the French author sometimes called the Father of Spiritualism.

One of the most important experiences I had occurred during the summer of 1962. I was reading the newspaper around 1:00 P.M. when suddenly, the figure of a middle-aged man appeared. He was thin with a pale white countenance. Neatly dressed in a white suit, he wore a gold watch chain like those used by gentlemen at the turn of the century. He smiled at me and bowed slightly. In spite of the bright sun angling through the wooden shutters, the image of the spirit sprang from a foggy atmosphere. The vision lasted about five or six seconds. When it faded, it looked like smoke dissipating.

Later that summer, I attended a meeting of the Federación de los Espiritistas de Puerto Rico (Federation of Spiritualists) in San Juan. I was the treasurer. I sat next to my charming friend, Doña Teresa Yañez, a poet and the first historian to write a book on the subject of Spiritualism on the Island of Puerto Rico.

It was my first visit to the organization's offices, so after greeting her, I looked at the pictures on the wall. Suddenly, my attention was drawn to the portrait of a distinguished gentleman, hanging at the very center of the front wall. He was the person whom I had seen a month ago in my home.

I asked Doña Teresa about him. She smiled and said that this gentleman had been a close friend of hers when she was a child and beginning her Spiritualism apprenticeship. He was a leader, an orator, and a homeopathic healer. The Center had been named after him.

Doña Teresa Yañez was an excellent medium, so I asked her why he had visited me.

"He likes you and is willing to help and guide you in your spiritual work," she answered.

These experiences proved to me that there is life after death and that the spirit world can approach us when necessary.

— *Jorge Quevedo, Ponce, Puerto Rico*
May 1997

Soldier at the Door

For four years when I was a child, my family lived in rural Kennesaw, Georgia, the site of a Civil War battle. The house had a long drive and a fenced yard. From the front door you could see the whole length of the drive. There were windows on each side of the door. We often heard a knocking at the door or the ringing of the doorbell, but when we answered it no one was there. One winter night in 1968, however, that changed.

My mother and I were home alone when the doorbell rang. We could see through the curtains that someone stood outside the door, but it was late and we were cautious. With the chain still on, we opened the door and saw a young man, blond and about 20 years old. He was wearing some sort of military uniform and a long gray overcoat. He looked disheveled and he was barefoot.

He asked for Jimmy and said that he had served with him in the war and that Jimmy had told him to come by if he was ever in town. My father, James Lloyd Thomas, had served in World War II — but everyone called him "Tommy."

My mother scolded the stranger, saying that he was too young to have served with my father, and she slammed the door.

As soon as the door was closed, we looked out the windows and saw that the young man was gone. He hadn't had time to make it down the drive. Although there was snow on the ground, there were no footprints anywhere.

Was he a wandering soldier from the fateful battle of Kennesaw Mountain, which took place only six miles from our house?
— *Barbara Healy, Belleville, Illinois*
November 1996

She Watches Over Us

In 1965, when I was five years old, I lived with my aunt Lena Mone and my grandfather Frank Bushee. I slept in my grandfather's bed because it was closer to the bathroom.

One night I woke up and had to go to the bathroom. I was afraid of the dark, and it took some courage to get up. When I finally did get up, I saw a woman standing in the doorway. She was big. Though a glow surrounded her, she was all dark, like a shadow.

I was afraid. I tried to wake up my grandfather, but he wouldn't stir. Then I got up and walked to the foot of the bed. The shadow just stood there.

"Who are you?" I asked her in a frightened voice. No answer. "Why don't you talk to me?" Still no answer.

When she didn't answer, it frightened me even more. I jumped back into bed and covered up my head. Soon I fell back to sleep.

I continued to see the mysterious woman night after night. I called her "grandfather's girlfriend" because she always stood at his bedroom door.

Only my grandfather believed me when I told them that I had seen her. One day he showed me some pictures he kept in his wallet. "Susan," he said, "if you see the woman that comes to my bedroom at night, just point to her."

We slowly looked at the pictures. Then I saw her and pointed to her. He asked if I knew who the woman was, and I told him it was his girlfriend who came to see him at night.

"No, this is your grandmother. She died before you were born." I was too young to understand, but my grandfather explained that my grandmother Sarah was not alive like we were, that she lived with

God, and the reason I saw her at night was that she came to make sure we were all right. He said she watched over us.

I asked him why she wouldn't talk to me. He said that she probably didn't want to frighten me more than I already was. I told him that it scared me nonetheless.

"Gramps, are you going to come back to me when you die?" I asked him.

"No, Susan, I will not come back, because when I die I will be with your grandmother and I'll be very happy. I wouldn't want to scare you, but I will watch over you along with your grandmother. So, you don't have to be afraid of me after I die."

My grandfather died in 1978 and he kept his word — he has never appeared to me. But I know he watches over me.

> — *Susan Bishop, Salem, New York*
> *October 1997*

The Death Coach

When I was growing up, we didn't question our elders, period! What they said was law, and if they told us something, it was true — because they said so! Therefore, when my father told me that he was of Welsh extraction and my mother told me that she came from French bloodlines I believed them. But it somehow never felt right. While my mother tended to cultivate friends of French extraction, preferred French cuisine, and praised French authors and movie actors, I was bored by it all. A child's reaction to too much sophistication? I honestly don't know. But I do know that I never felt French.

Mother had always been proud of the spelling of her first name, Maire, and said that it was a French form of Mary. She read French and spoke a little, which she said she learned from her mother and grandmother, who was supposed to have been an orphaned indentured servant from France. When I entered high school she requested that I take French. It was there that I learned that the French form of

Mary is Marie. Something clicked in the back of my mind, but I didn't know what to do about it.

When my father passed away a few years later I came across some of my mother's papers while helping her go through his legal affairs. They bore some decidedly non-French names. When I commented on this fact my mother hastily took the papers and put them away. I thought that perhaps she might not be full-blooded French, but because the matter seemed so important to her, I dropped it.

As the years passed, she developed a serious heart condition. I moved into her house to take care of her. At first she rallied, but eventually the medication stopped working and her doctors decided that surgery was out of the question. It was only a matter of time. On December 7, 1992, my mother had a massive coronary. I stayed with her in the hospital for most of the next few days. On the night of February 10, my husband insisted that I come home with him to get some rest. Once in my own bed, I fell into a deep sleep.

In the early morning, I was awakened by the sound of snorting horses and pounding hooves. I opened my eyes and saw a black coach drawn by black-plumed horses. The coach came toward me through the bedroom, then slowed to a stop. I heard the impatient scrape of the horses' hooves as they pawed the ground, bobbing their heads, and I saw icy breath snorting from their nostrils. The driver, dressed in black and wearing a top hat, was Death himself!

I felt a terrible fear as he turned to look right at me — as if to make sure that I saw him. At that moment, even as I shrank away, I understood that I was in no danger. I knew that my mother's soul was inside his coach. Then the driver snapped the reins and rode away.

My heart was pounding. I shook my husband awake. I immediately called the hospital and was told that my mother had passed away only minutes before.

My husband, who has some Native American blood, accepted this all matter-of-factly. My mother, he said, had simply come to say goodbye.

That was all well and good, except that I had heard that the death coach, like the Banshee, was only supposed to come for the souls of the Irish. Being of Irish extraction was something that had never occurred to me, and my mother, with her condescending way, looked down on the Irish as "common."

I began doing a little digging. I amassed family death certificates, marriage certificates, and census records. Nothing indicated that my mother's family came from France. Names that my mother remembered proved not even to be in our family. Places where she said her family had lived were nonexistent. I wrote to several heritage societies, asking if any of their members recognized the unusual surname Ogle. No one had heard of the name. Then on March 13, 1996, the Celtic Research Society confirmed that my grandfather was Irish. I was thrilled: My long search was over.

Why my mother hid her roots, I do not know. Barring another other-worldly visitation, I probably will never know. I believe the death coach really does appear to those of Irish descent — sometimes even before you know that you are Irish!

— *Elizabeth Phillips-Miravallen*
October 1997

The Haunted Hollow

When I moved to this beautiful, wild, Ozark hill country in 1983, my favorite pastime became cruising the back roads where the heart of the country reveals its loveliest vistas. It was on just such a road where I met my friend Lee. Lost Creek Hollow Road.

It was a mild spring afternoon, the sun was shining, and the Ozark dogwoods decorated the woods with their snowy white blooms. I was driving along, enjoying the scenery, when I came upon the most beautiful house I had ever seen. It was a house of beautiful coral pink rocks, set in a wooded clearing.

I stopped in front of the house and sat in my pickup truck, mesmerized, until a woman emerged from the house to check me out. Her name was Lee. She lived alone, like me, although she had not started out that way.

"I moved here with my husband, Ted, from New York City," Lee told me over coffee. "He was retired from the construction business. We bought this old, ramshackle house on 65 acres and promptly began remodeling it. But Ted died of a heart attack halfway into the project. So there I was, a 55-year-old woman with an unfinished house, in the middle of the most beautiful nowhere in the world. What was I going to do?"

"Well, you obviously decided to stay," I said. "Who finished the house?"

"I did. But I had help," Lee continued. "I don't tell this to many people, because it's such an unbelievable story. But it happens to be true. After Ted died, I cried myself to sleep for weeks, until the night when Ted came to me in my dream. He told me he would help me finish the house. And that's what he did." Lee explained that Ted appeared in her dreams nightly, telling her what project to tackle next and giving her instructions. Then, when she did the work, Lee swears that she could feel an invisible pair of hands guiding her own. So it continued until the entire house was finished to perfection.

I believed Lee's story.

In February 1987, Lee was visiting her daughter and new grandchild in New York City. On the second day of her absence I had a phone call from a neighbor of hers, informing me that Lee's beautiful house had burned to the ground overnight. I knew it would break her heart.

Three days later, four teenagers confessed. They said they had broken in and were helping themselves to soda when they were scared out of their wits by an indignant ghost who slammed doors, banged on walls, and turned the lights on and off.

"We got out of there pretty fast after that," one of the boys told the sheriff. "But we went back the next night and set the house on fire."

Lee, heartbroken, moved back to New York. She has sold the land several times now, but it always seems to come back to her when the new owners say there is something strange about the property, stop paying on it, and leave.

— *Renie Burghardt, Doniphan, Missouri*
September 1997

Ghost Story

I moved to an apartment in Sherman Oaks, California, and felt lucky to have found such a beautiful place. Though the apartments were 30 years old, they had been kept in perfect shape.

After I was settled in, however, I felt many times that I wasn't alone. Sometimes I looked through the bedrooms and closets, sure I would find someone, but no one was there.

One night I worked late and didn't get home until 4:00 a.m. When I got to bed at 4:30, it was still dark. I knew daybreak wasn't far away and the light from the bedroom down the hall would awaken me too early. As I lay in bed, wondering whether to go in the other bedroom and close the drapes or just close the door, I saw the outline of a figure in the hall, slowly coming my way.

The figure was outlined by the streetlight shining in the windows of the other bedroom. I sat up in bed and watched as it came to the foot of my bed and stood there.

I was scared. I had read ghost stories, but I had always attributed them to someone's overactive imagination. Now, however, I apologize. They are real!

I said to the figure, "I think you lived here before I did. I don't know what happened, but I live here now. You are dead and you must go to the next plane. Follow the light and you will find God. You are finished with this life. Find the light and God bless you."

The ghost turned around slowly and walked away. When it got to the door, it stopped and seemed to look back. Then it continued down the hall and faded away.

I got up, turned on all the lights and the television, and completely fell apart. I waited until 8:00 and knocked on my nearest neighbor's door. After her surprised look and questions, I asked her to tell me about the people who had lived in the apartment before me.

"An old couple," she said, "very devoted to each other, moved in when the apartments were new and lived there more than 30 years. He was 90 years old and she was 83. They both were terminally ill, in pain, and waiting to die."

One night my neighbor had heard a gunshot, soon followed by a second. Then she had called the police. Perhaps, together, the couple had decided to end the pain. They left no notes.

The neighbor didn't know who had shot whom, but based on my ghostly experience, one of them had remained earthbound. I hoped my words helped reunite them.

I reluctantly stayed in that apartment for three more months, but I never saw the ghost again.

— *Flossie Mahan, San Bernardino, California*
September 1997

Mother's Love

Mom was overly protective of me since I — as her change of life baby — had been a fragile child often in poor health. In 1948, after recovering from polio that almost killed me, I was left with an unusual complication. For no discernable reason, I began to die from time to time. This strange attack started with a shortness of breath followed by a sudden closing of my throat, as if someone were strangling me. Sometimes this happened as I slept, leaving Mom in a constant state of worry.

One night when I was 14, the worst attack came while I slept. It brought me to the edge of death. The only thing that saved me had been Mom hearing my "death rattle" as she had walked past my room. Mom frantically rubbed my arms and legs and yelled at me to wake up while Dad called the doctor. I could feel myself slipping out of my body. I had no feeling in my body, but I could hear my parents talking. When the doctor arrived, he gave me a shot and within a half hour, I was back in my body, feeling perfectly normal.

"There is nothing physically wrong with your daughter," the doctor told Mom. "I don't know what caused this attack. I don't even know if my treatment ended it. I feel that it will happen again, maybe tomorrow, maybe next year. I also feel that when it happens again, it will kill her."

Mom had spent the last three years of her life in constant worry about my condition. The day before she died in 1958, she promised to continue watching over me for as long as I needed her.

My attacks ended as mysteriously as they had begun within a week after Mom's death. Eventually, I forgot about them.

In 1988, my attacks began to reappear about every six months, sometimes with enough strength to send me to the emergency room.

After examining and treating me, the emergency room doctors all said the same thing: "There is nothing physically wrong with you. I don't know what caused this attack. I don't even know if my treatment ended it." All of the doctors were surprised at how quickly I recovered.

In October 1995, I awoke one night to the sound of Mom's voice calling me. Forcing my eyes open, I saw her standing over me.

"Maggie," Mom said, "Wake up. You're dying. Wake up. Now!"

I suddenly realized I was having another attack. I couldn't breath. Even worse, I couldn't move. Panic hit me as I realized I was strangling to death and was unable to help myself. Mom continued calling to me, commanding me to sit up. I forced myself up on one arm and felt the tightness begin to leave my throat. At first I could only gasp for air, but slowly I began breathing normally. After what seemed like an eternity, the attack ended.

I looked again at Mom and watched her begin to disappear. "Thanks, Mom," I said. For one short second, I saw her familiar smile, then she was gone.

Ever since then, I have felt a special bonding with my mother, one that is stronger than when she was still alive.

— *Margaret L. Cooper, Jacksonville, Florida*
November 1997

The Three Lights

When my mother, Shirley Marsh Aulenbacher, was young she lived in Waterford, Pennsylvania. Three of her cousins — triplet girls — died when they were three years old.

When the girls' mother came home from the burial services, she fell asleep in her living room. As night came on, she was awakened by the laughter of small children in the yard. She crept out on her porch and looked about.

She saw three blue lights lingering near the swings. Then she recognized the voices as those belonging to her girls. They were laughing and having a good time together.

Then the lights swung out toward the corn field and headed to the cemetery, which was not far from her home. She followed the lights for a long time and eventually understood that her beautiful daughters had come to show their love for her.

My mother believed that beings from the spirit world are here to love us and help us through hard times.

— *Shirley Renner, Girard, Pennsylvania*
November 1997

Relatively Speaking

When my daughter Emily was only a year old, in 1993, she usually slept soundly through the night and didn't wake up until she heard the rest of the family moving around. Normally, I tried to keep the house quiet until her breakfast was ready at 7:00 or 8:00.

Around 6:00 one morning, however, I woke to the sound of voices. I checked to see if my clock radio had gone off, but it hadn't. I checked my four-year-old's room, which was next to mine. It was quiet. The voices seemed to be coming from Emily's room at the end of the hall.

Her door was shut, so before I disturbed her I checked the rest of the house. There was no sound in the living room, or the kitchen, or the basement. I now was certain the voices were coming from the baby's room.

For some reason, I didn't feel alarmed. I stood outside her door for a moment, listening. It sounded like there were five or six adults in the room: Two or three women were apparently cooing at the baby, while in the background two or three men seemed to be talking among themselves. I couldn't understand what they were saying, though — because they were speaking some sort of Scandinavian language.

Suddenly, it dawned on me: My great-grandmother had died just a few weeks before, at the age of 99. She had emigrated to the Midwest from Denmark as a young woman, and had never seen most of her 13 brothers and sisters again. I simply knew that she had come back to see the baby — and to show her off to some of her long-lost relatives.

After a moment, I reached out to open the door — and just as my hand touched the knob, the voices stopped. I peeked in, and Emily was standing in her crib, wide awake, staring into the middle of the room. She was too young to tell me what she had seen — but since then, the voices have returned a few times, and both of my daughters have heard them, too. We don't mind. We know it's just Grandma, stopping in to check on us.

— *Corrine Alkofer, St. Paul, Minnesota*
September 1997

The Legend of Screaming Charlie

FATE

True Reports of the Strange and Unknown
The World's Leading Magazine of the Paranormal

Psychic Kids
Help Your Children
Develop ESP

How to Hear
Spirit Voices

The Cult of
Joanna Southcott

Each Month, Leave Your World Behind ...
and Enter the Unknown Realms of

FATE

For almost 50 years, FATE has given you what no one
else has: the latest-breaking events, evidence, and discoveries in
the world of the supernatural. We don't rehash the same old
stories and theories you've heard for years. With FATE you get
up-to-date reports that keep you on the cutting edge of the
paranormal. Don't miss even one spellbinding month of the
boldest, most exciting exploration of the strange and unknown
available in this galaxy — subscribe today!

Save 49% off the cover price of $42.
YOU SAVE $20.50! Just call:

(800) 728-2730

GRAVE'S END
A True Ghost Story
Elaine Mercado, Foreword by Hans Holzer

A first-person account of a haunted house in Brooklyn and the family that lived there . . .

When Elaine Mercado and her first husband bought their home in Brooklyn, N.Y., in 1982, they had no idea that they and their two young daughters were embarking on a 13-year nightmare. Within a few days of moving in, elaine began to have the sensation of being watched. Soon her oldest daughter Karen felt it too, and they began hearing scratching noises and noticing weird smells. After they remodeled the basement into Karin's bedroom, the strange happenings increased, especially after Karin and her friends explored the crawl space under the house. In the attic they sometimes saw a very small woman dressed as a bride, and on the stairs they would see a young man. Then the "suffocating dreams" started. Yet her husband refused to sell the house.

This book is the true story of how one family tried to adjust to living in a haunted house. It also tells how, with the help of parapsychologist Dr. Hans Holzer and medium Marisa Anderson, they discovered the identity of the ghosts and were able to assist them to the "light."

0-7387-0003-7, 6 x 9, 192 pp.   **$12.95**

MESSAGES AND MIRACLES
Estraordinary Experiences of the Bereaved
Louis E. LaGrand, Ph.D.

In this moving and compassionate work, one of the pioneers in after-death communication (ADC) research explores the reasons why ADCs occur and how they help the bereaved.

Based on his counseling experience, interviews with numerous people who have had contact with a deceased loved one, and the many questions people have asked him since the the release of his first book, *After Death Communication*, LaGrand unfolds an untapped source of support for the bereaved and those who attempt to comfort them.

Learn whether contact experience is simply the stress of bereavement or an authentic communication, how it can help you establish a new relationship with the deceased, and how to talk to children who report the experience. Read actual accounts of ADCs which have never before appeared in print.

1-56718-406-5, 336 pp., 6 x 9, illus. $12.95

INSTANT PALM READER
A Roadmap to Life
Linda Domin

Etched upon your palm is an aerial view of all the scenes you will travel in the course of your lifetime. Your characteristics, skills and abilities are imprinted in your mind and transferred as images onto your hand. Now, with this simple, flip-through pictorial guide, you can assemble your own personal palm reading, like a professional, almost instantly.

The *Instant Palm Reader* shows you how your hands contain the picture of the real you—physically, emotionally and mentally. More than 500 easy-to-read diagrams will provide you with candid, uplifting revelations about yourself: personality, childhood, career, finances, family, love life, talents and destiny.

With the sensitive information artfully contained within each interpretation, you will also be able to uncover your hidden feelings and unconscious needs as you learn the secrets of this 3,000-year-old science.

1-56718-232-1, 6 x 9, 288 pp., 500 illus., softcover $14.95

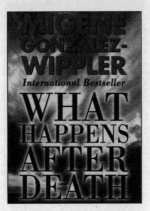

WHAT HAPPENS AFTER DEATH
Scientific & Personal Evidence for Survival
Migene González-Wippler

What does science tell us about life after death? How do the different religions explain the mystery? What is the answer given by the strange mystical science known as Spiritism? These and other questions about the life beyond are explored in *What Happens After Death*.

The first part of the book is an objective study of the research about life after death. The second part is a personal narrative by a spirit guide named Kirkudian about his various incarnations. While the two sections could be considered two separate books, they simply express the same concepts in uniquely different ways.

Experience for yourself one soul's journey through the afterlife, and discover the ultimate truth: that every soul is created in union with all other souls, and that we are all manifestations of one purpose.

1-56718-327-1, 5 3/16 x 8, 256 pp., softcover $7.95

IS YOUR PET PSYCHIC?
Developing Psychic Communication With Your Pet
Richard Webster

What Is Your Pet Thinking?

Cats who predict earthquakes, dogs who improve marriages, and horses who can add and subtract—animals have long been known to possess amazing talents. Now you can experience for yourself the innate psychic abilities of your pet with *Is Your Pet Psychic.*

Learn to exchange ideas with your pet that will enhance your relationship in many ways. Transmit and receive thoughts when you're at a distance, help lost pets find their way home, even communicate with pets who are deceased.

Whether your animal walks, flies, or swims, it is possible to establish a psychic bond and a more meaningful relationship. This book is full of instructions, as well as true case studies from past and present.

0-7387-0193-9, 5 ³⁄₁₆ X 8, 288 pp., bibliog, index $12.95

UFO FBI CONNECTION
The Secret History of the Government's Cover-up
Bruce S. Maccabee, Ph.D.

UFO-FBI Connection details the existence of the "real X-Files"—knowledge held by the FBI and the U.S. Air Force on UFO sightings between the years 1947 to 1954, and withheld from the media and the public. Often filed under the title "Flying Discs: Security Matter-X," this information is revealed here, for the first time ever in any book.

The FBI and CIA records highlight the inconsistencies between the Air Force's public denial of UFO activity and what top officials already believed: that UFOs were real, unexplainable objects that could not be explained away as natural phenomena, hoaxes, or U.S. or Soviet experimental aircraft.

1-56718-493-6, 336 pp., 6 x 9, photos   **$14.95**

PSYCHIC PETS & SPIRIT ANIMALS
True Stories from the Files of FATE Magazine
FATE Magazine Editorial Staff

In spite of all our scientific knowledge about animals, important questions remain about the nature of animal intelligence. Now, a large body of personal testimony compels us to raise still deeper questions. Are some animals, like some people, psychic? If human beings survive death, do animals? Do bonds exist between people and animals that are beyond our ability to comprehend?

Psychic Pets & Spirit Animals is a varied collection from the past 50 years of the real-life experiences of ordinary people with creatures great and small. You will encounter psychic pets, ghost animals, animal omens, extraordinary human-animal bonds, pet survival after death, phantom protectors and the weird creatures of cryptozoology.

The true stories in *Psychic Pets & Spirit Animals* suggest that animals are, in many ways, more like us than we think—and that they, too, can step into the strange and unknowable realm of the paranormal, where all things are possible.

ISBN: 1-56718-299-2, 272 pp., softcover $4.99